LIAR

ROB ROBERGE

CROWN PUBLISHERS
NEW YORK

LIAR

A MEMOIR

Library of Congress Cataloging-in-Publication Data
Roberge, Rob.
    Liar : a memoir / Rob Roberge.—First edition.
        pages   cm
        1. Roberge, Rob—Mental health. 2. Manic-depressive persons—
United States—Biography. 3. Drug addicts—United States—
Biography. 4. Mental illness—Treatment—United States. 5. Drug
abuse—Treatment—United States. I. Title.
    RC516.R63 2015
    616.89'50092—dc23
    [B]   2015018970

ISBN 978-0-553-44806-1
eBook ISBN 978-0-553-44807-8

PRINTED IN THE UNITED STATES OF AMERICA

Book design by Anna Thompson
Jacket design by Jake Nicolella
Jacket photograph by David Ryle / Getty Images

10 9 8 7 6 5 4 3 2 1

First Edition

FOR ALL THOSE WHO LOVED ME
WHEN I HAD TROUBLE DOING SO MYSELF

But remember, also, young man: you are not the first person who has been alone and alone.

—F. SCOTT FITZGERALD

Meaning isn't made only in a moment but in how it is processed over a lifetime.

—GINA FRANGELLO

LIAR

1

1977: You have your first girlfriend and you are, as far as your ten-year-old self knows, madly in love. You are Nicole's "buddy" in science class—that's how you meet, because she is a bright girl who has been advanced a grade and she needs an older student to help her fit in. And the principal—a man who knows you incredibly well from your frightening number of trips to his office—seems to have decided that it might be good for you to be responsible for once. To take care of someone and not get in trouble.

You and Nicole pass notes in class with questions like *Do you like me?* with "Yes" and "No" boxes. You hold hands in the coatroom. Instead of teaching her to behave, you teach her that the more you misbehave, the less adult supervision you tend to have. Screw up and you are out back clapping erasers together. Screw up even worse and you get sent to the coatroom. Really screw up and you get to read books together in the library.

On your eleventh birthday, she is killed in the woods that back three or four neighborhood developments. Woods that you all played in.

You try to think about what she looked like, but you really have no memories of this. You remember two long brown pigtails, but you could be getting those from her picture now on an Unsolved Murders in CT website, in her last school picture ever, taken the year she was killed. She wears a white-and-red print dress. She has brown eyes that match her hair, which is pulled into two shoulder-length pigtails. She has a posed but happy smile. That photo has replaced your actual memory. You think of her now, you see that picture that everyone else can see.

In the woods, Nicole's head was crushed with a large rock. "Bludgeoned" is the word the newspapers use, and you have to look up the word and it will remain your most vivid memory of finding a definition in a dictionary. You are old enough to realize none of this can be your fault, but you remember the principal telling you that your job is to "take care" of Nicole and the phrase will not leave your head no matter how much you want it to.

For years, you think (there were rumors, after all) she was raped and then *bludgeoned*. She was never raped, you find out much later. Though, for so many years in your head, she *was*—the facts, for years, were not the truth. You only learn she wasn't raped when you try to research her case in your early forties—thinking, somehow, that it might help your life make sense if you could make some sense of her death.

From that day in 1977, you never—especially until you leave your hometown at eighteen—look at a man without thinking, *It could be him*. Every coach. Every teacher. Every strange man who ever walks by you. For years you're horrified whenever you're left alone with a man. Sometimes, without warning, you flush with rage and want to hurt some guy you've never seen before. Your reaction to everything in the world starts to frighten you.

Her case remains unsolved thirty-five years later. It will never be resolved and it won't reduce itself to meaning. She has been gone from this earth nearly five times as long as she was here and sometimes—even though you have known hundreds of people better—you think that relationship may be the most formative one of your life. While many things happened before Nicole was killed, this is really where all the other things start and, to a certain degree, end.

1974: Your parents throw a party on a Saturday night. You sit at the top of the stairs listening to their music, their laughter, and the clinking of bottles and ice in a bucket. Smell the cigarette smoke. They play Bob Dylan and Johnny Cash records all night long.

The next morning, while your parents are sleeping, you're in the basement looking at all the different colors of liquor in the different-sized glasses. You drink them, one by one, a red one first because you tend to like red foods and red candy, so why not red drinks? It tastes fine. Not as good as, say, Hi-C, but a few minutes in, you feel better than you ever have in your life, except for that accidental overdose two years ago on some pill at the mental institution where your father works.

A beautiful new world floods through you. You smoke half cigarettes from ashtrays. You know you have to feel like this again.

From this day forward, if you are not high, you are not happy.

FALL 1985: You and your girlfriend Sasha have broken up. No one understands the kind of pain you are in. Your pain and loneliness are undocumented in the history of human pain and loneliness.

All day and all night, you lie on your bed with your Walkman on your chest and Bob Dylan's *Blood on the Tracks* playing as loud as the machine can go into your headphones. Your eyes are closed. You don't move except to smoke cigarettes or drink beer. One side of the tape plays to the end and you open up the Walkman and flip the tape and listen to the other side.

You do this for weeks. Your life is over. You will never know love again—of that much you are sure. Friends try to get you to come out. To drink. To party. To talk. If you had enough money, you *might* go see the friends of yours who sell Percocet and morphine, but you don't have the money so why bother seeing those people?

You ignore them all and get wasted and smoke and listen to Bob Dylan because, really, only Bob Dylan has any idea of the amount of pain you are in.

Only you and Bob Dylan have ever known this kind of love and only you and Bob Dylan have ever known what it's like to lose this kind of love.

FALL 1984: You are diagnosed as bipolar with rapid cycling and occasional psychotic episodes. You've been up for almost a week and you don't remember any of what a friend later tells you that you said and did the last two or three days you were awake. It's like a drunken blackout, but longer and worse, since apparently you were acting "pretty full-blown crazy," according to your friend. He's a few years older than you and his ex-wife is a schizophrenic. He thinks you may be one too. He convinces you to see the college psychiatrist, who sends you somewhere else, and that doctor tells you that you have been self-medicating— for years, from what you say.

The good news is you are not schizophrenic. The bad news is you *are* pretty full-blown crazy. From this point on, for a decade or so, you will only tell people very close to you that it's possible they might have to take you to a hospital someday. That you won't want to let them and that they have to ignore whatever you say at those times. This makes even the people closest to you tense and nervous about what it means to love you. And you will hate yourself for it.

The doctor puts you on medicines you can't pronounce and tells you that, no matter what you do, you should not drink alcohol with them, you shouldn't do any recreational drugs, and, especially, that you should *never*, "with a brain like yours," take any hallucinogens like acid, mescaline, or mushrooms again. When you're released, you take his medicine, but you don't really stop taking your drugs. You *do* try to slow down. But only because you are afraid he's right and you could go fully insane. A week after the appointment, you drop acid and hang out in the Boston Common playing your guitar for hours.

He's right. His medicine and your drugs don't go together at all. Your drugs make you feel better. The ones the doctor puts you on make you feel stupid and like someone packed your brain in icy gauze. Like someone has taken a cold wet mop and swirled it gray over your mind.

You no longer have weeks where you stay awake for days and feel great, like your brain is working several times faster than it normally does. You sleep all the time, but you never feel rested. Your feet shuffle—you don't lift them when you walk. You answer questions really slowly. You can barely play the guitar. Friends ask you what's wrong.

Before the month is out, the doctor's medicine stays in your bathroom and you never refill the script. The people who move into the apartment after you will find these pills to be the only ones you left behind.

AUGUST 20, 2009: You are going to kill yourself. You're a year into your relapse, after nearly fifteen years clean, and you're a liar—you've lied to almost everyone you know. You are, yet again, the person you used to be. The man you despised. It's come down to two choices: You can either be a junkie or you can clean up and be the person you were for fifteen years. Cleaning up seems impossible. The thought of walking into an AA meeting and taking a newcomer chip makes you sick with shame.

Which leaves being a junkie. And you've spent enough time in meetings to know where that ends:

- Jail
- Institutions
- Death

You're forty-three years old. You've been a college professor, a good husband, a good friend, an honest person. The disgrace of being arrested for heroin would burn even worse than taking a newcomer chip. Everyone would know. Shame is an endless white noise of pain in your head. You're confused and overwhelmed and you are as alone as you have ever felt.

You can't go to rehab. You can't admit your weakness to anyone, even though you know, god you know—what addict doesn't?—that addiction's not about intelligence and it's not about strength. Your whole life has been a lesson in this: Knowing something may make it a fact, but feeling something makes it a truth. And the truth is you are trapped. You have nowhere left to go that doesn't make you feel like your life has added up, in the end and despite some great moments, to you being a loser who just can't stay clean. Who can't keep people happy. Who can't function in this world. You're done. Defeated.

Too many days have shown themselves to be this. Your life from now on. No matter how many people may have once loved you, no matter how many you may once have loved, at the bottom is this: You are rotten at the core and you cannot be fixed. You will forever be broken.

You've tried living clean. Now you've just ended up worse than where you started.

So you decide to kill yourself. To exert the last control you have left. At least you will die loaded and it might feel good. You feel guilty for thinking this. You've been squirreling away oxycodone and Xanax for the last month, keeping yourself on a maintenance dose in an effort not to be sick. It's almost impossible to resist the temptation to get high, but you have a plan: Once you have gathered more than enough pills for an overdose, you are going out to a shack in Wonder Valley and you're going to kill yourself there.

You're going to shred all your ID; you're going to take the plates off your car, toss them into the desert, and park far away from the shack and hope that by the time someone finds your body rotting in the desert months or hopefully years later, there will be no way to tell who you were. Your wife will never have to know that you killed yourself. You've picked up the emotional messes of suicides before—nothing ever helps someone recover from that. Putting her through that is out of the question. You can't hang yourself for her to find. You can't eat a gun. You, both for your own chickenshit reasons of wanting to die happily loaded for one last time and because you never want your wife, Gayle, discovering your body, have made different, elaborate plans.

Of course, you haven't *really* thought it through. You're

exhausted at the thought of living another day, and you are in a fog of drugs. They could probably ID your body from all your broken bones or your dental records, even though you've only been to a dentist once in seventeen years. Even if your body is totally decomposed and your fingerprints are gone. Plus, just disappearing on a person after fifteen years of marriage is not exactly a way to leave her without a wound that wouldn't heal. But you are not in your right mind.

At this point, you're having trouble getting high. Only a large enough dosage that brings you close to an OD anyway is good enough to catch a buzz. It takes about four hundred milligrams of opiates to get even a little high and about two hundred over the course of a day to stave off dopesickness. You have saved well over a thousand milligrams, plus almost thirty Xanax, and you figure this will do the job.

You get to the Wonder Valley shack. You love Wonder Valley—you own a cabin out there where you go to write and relax, or at least you used to. It's the quietest place you have ever known. You want to die somewhere beautiful. You've chosen an abandoned house you actually like, one you have history with. You once made a short film with a scene shot here. A friend who was in the movie is now dead from a lifetime of drug use and you think of him. You dreamed of him all the time after his death, almost every night for about six months, but you haven't for more than a year now. You were still managing life then—something that seems impossible now.

The shack has five rooms: what used to be someone's

kitchen, a living room, three bedrooms. You sit in the living room, littered with years of pigeon shit and graffiti on whatever drywall is left. Almost every one of the hundreds of abandoned shacks in Wonder Valley are missing doors and the birds scatter as you walk into the shack. The ceiling is mostly gone—open to the rafters and wood and corrugated metal patches on the roof. Above you is a piece of what you figure has to be a bit of misspelled graffiti: JESUS LOVES AL. Unless it was written by some guy named Al. It reminds you of the misspelled tattoos you've known in life—a guy in a Florida drunk tank with "I Eat Pusy" on his arm. A guy—also in Florida, perhaps the state of misspelled tats—who meant to have "Unbridled" on his stomach but had somehow managed "Unbirdled."

You sit, your back to the wall with the fewest shit stains, though you wonder why it matters now. Wind blows through the sagebrush and ground cover and pigeons slowly return and perch on the rafters. Only a few at first, then maybe thirty. You try counting them, but they move a lot and you keep losing track around the low twenties. You're feeling slightly manic and noises are starting to sound like murmuring voices. You wonder briefly if you're in the start of an episode, and that maybe this isn't the day to kill yourself. That you can't trust yourself in this state. But, even if it is an episode, you're not yet having any hallucinations. You're frighteningly clearheaded. You're certain you're ready to die. You listen to the wind. You have seventeen cigarettes left. A ziplock baggie of pills bulging in your jeans. You have been here half an hour. You have time.

You're not debating anything with yourself. You just figure, what's the hurry? Pay some attention to the world. All this will be gone soon. You think about Gayle. You hear her saying that the only thing she would never forgive you for is killing yourself. She couldn't understand where you are and where you've been. You're sorry, but not sorry enough, really. It's your life. Plus, she said that before she had a junkie husband. She doesn't know what you are or who you are anymore. You smoke a cigarette down to the end and flick it out toward the front door—or where the front door would be if there was a door. You miss. It lands on an old phone book, and you hope it doesn't light the shack on fire and draw fast attention from any firefighters who might save you, but then you remember phone books don't burn easily, which you know from cleaning your compulsively hoarding grandmother's house after her death and you saw she'd tried to burn one in the fireplace for heat she could no longer afford.

APRIL 15, 1912: The *Titanic* sinks on its maiden voyage. There are enough lifeboats for more than half the people on board yet fewer than a third make it to them. Just over seven hundred people survive, making it one of the most witnessed disasters in history up to that point.

When asked later, more than ninety percent of the surviving women reply that they were on the final lifeboat launched—an overwhelming statistical impossibility given that nearly four hundred women survived and the largest of the lifeboats held seventy people.

Both the United States and Great Britain hold massive inquiries into the disaster, relying on eyewitness testimony for many of their conclusions. At the British inquiry, each survivor is asked how many people were lowered into each lifeboat. The *minimum* estimates are then taken—some estimates being nearly twice as high as the lowest ones—and the testimony of the most conservative witnesses offered these numbers:

- Number of people lowered into lifeboats, by minimum estimates: 107 crew, 43 men, and 704 women and children. Total: 854
- Actual number of people lowered into lifeboats: 139 crew, 119 men, and 393 women and children. Total: 651

Seventy percent more men and forty-five percent fewer women made it to safety than the most conservative eyewitnesses had testified. And twenty-five percent fewer people were on the boats—only 651 survivors actually boarded lifeboats. Very few of the eyewitness testimonies were much like any of the others in a wide range of small details and some enormous details, such as the fact that witnesses were conflicted on whether or not the 882-foot ship broke entirely in half prior to sinking.

No one came to the inquiry to lie. No one intentionally avoided telling the truth. But if the initial fact is the true event, that initial truth then becomes like a sophisticated virus that adapts to each host, so that it is never quite identical to the original virus, nor to its manifestations in any other host.

DECEMBER 25, 2009: Singer/songwriter Vic Chesnutt—a quadriplegic dating from a car accident while driving drunk at the age of eighteen—dies of an overdose of muscle relaxants at the age of forty-five. It is ruled a suicide. Prior to his death, in an interview with *Fresh Air* host Terry Gross, Chesnutt claims to have "attempted suicide three or four times . . . It didn't take." He says he guesses he was, those times, too chicken to go through with it.

2009: The doctors tell you you've had at least seven major concussions over the course of your life. Three or four when you were a basketball player in high school before drugs and a knee torn in three places brought what was left of your athletic career to a close.

A few more came in car accidents, one so bad it fractured your neck—a hairline, but apparently dangerous and close enough to the spinal cord that you are lucky you can walk or move your arms. You came, a doctor tells you years later—when you have insurance and get MRIs and the full workup for your years of blinding, debilitating migraines—incredibly close to being a quadriplegic when you were twenty-three.

"When did you break your neck?" the doctor says.

"I don't think I did."

He points to the fracture and taps it with the end of his pen. You hear his pen make a ticking sound on the X-ray and the glass behind it. "Another centimeter and you'd be answering me by blinking your eyes once for yes and two for no."

"So, does that explain my headaches?" you say.

The doctor tells you it explains some of the headaches and he sits you down and tells you about post-concussion syndrome and a possible condition known as CTE. A condition they cannot diagnose until they perform an autopsy, so whether or not you have it is a guess. He tells you about your possible risk for early dementia and the loss of the control of your frontal lobe and the loss of your memory. "To be clear," he tells you, "there's no guarantee you'll have dementia. It's just that your odds are a good deal higher than the average person."

You are a writer. Hell, you are a human being. You *are* your memories. Take away a person's memories and they may as well be brain-dead. This scares you more than anything. To slowly disappear in front of your wife's and your friends' eyes. To have come this far to be able to love and enjoy life and truly be worthy of other people's love after so many years of trying to destroy yourself. To know that someone else is more important than you and that she would have to watch this—watch what makes you what and who you are slip away by degrees like the tide going out.

You will become someone who is Not You. You will forget when you met your wife. You will forget the look in her eyes and her smile where one eye closes more than the other, that beautiful asymmetry. You will forget the terror you felt seeing her fear when she went into emergency surgery and you thought it was the beginning of the end and you decided, calmly, that you would kill yourself if she died.

You will lose every bad and every beautiful moment of your life and you will cease to exist.

You will, you promise yourself—before you lose everything you remember—before you forget how much you love the people you love, kill yourself, which wouldn't be a suicide because you would never be yourself again anyway. This would just be dying on your own terms.

The worst part will not be the total loss at the end. It will be the start—when you still know who you are, and you know what, and who, you are losing.

Sometimes you aren't thinking about it and then it hits you. You make lists, you write down everything you can remember. You try not to think about the fact that all of these could be nothing other than stories you might read someday as if they happened to a stranger, because you might be that stranger someday. Your memories are already foggy and scrambled at times. And then, they may not even be there anymore.

This, you worry about. Always.

JULY 28, 1841: The body of "Beautiful Cigar Girl" Mary Rogers is found in the Hudson River. The murder remains unsolved and becomes a national news story, inspiring Edgar Allan Poe's "The Mystery of Marie Rogêt" a year later.

SOMETIME IN THE '80s: The last thing you remember, you are drinking at Father's Five—a bar on Mass Ave in Boston, and you put Jason and the Scorchers' astounding cover of Dylan's "Absolutely Sweet Marie" on the jukebox. Then you wake up in an apartment in Montreal—a city where you know exactly no one, including the guy whose apartment you are in, and he looks at you the way you might look at a unfamiliar sweater that someone left on your floor after a party.

You take a beer from his fridge and drink it in the stairwell on your way down to the street. A normal person might freak out. *You* might have freaked out only a year or two ago. Instead, you are only pissed off that you don't have enough money to get drunk right then and that you have to hitchhike back to Boston. Even your friends or girlfriends, tolerant as they are—more saints than you can count on both hands, actually—are not going to come pick you up hundreds of miles away. Some things are too much to ask, after all.

1985: You have a dorm room with your own bed but you end up sleeping with Melissa every night for a few months. Sleeping with—but not having sex. Melissa is a lesbian. But she's single. You start as a friend who helps her with her guitar. You're a better guitar player than she is, but she is a much better songwriter and singer.

At night, the two of you drink and play guitar. She's a Beatles fanatic. You teach her all the early singles. You teach her the dual lead harmony parts on "And Your Bird Can Sing."

With the lights out, you drink and smoke cigarettes and hold each other while the rain patters on the roof of your dorm. You are young—you know nothing—and you wonder sometimes if the power of pure love (because you're pretty sure that's what you're feeling) could make Melissa love you the way you love her. In the years to come, you'll sleep with people and next to people, but you will never again this often fall asleep holding on to someone and waking up still holding them the next morning.

You know the smell of her hair. The pace of her breathing. The way her right hand tremors for no known reason while she's deep in sleep. She lets you kiss her eyelids, but not her lips.

"We don't want to get confused here," she says. Too late, you think but don't say.

You play in a band called Junkyard—Junkyard sounds like every member in the band fell in love with the same Johnny Thunders record, which is pretty much the case. Even your originals sound like covers. Melissa plays in a band of four women who all dress in black and have on pale makeup. They call themselves the Bell Jars. Their originals sound great and even their covers sound original. They are the real deal. Junkyard is not.

The Bell Jars have a show coming up at the Rat—a major Boston club in Kenmore Square. Melissa is worried about her guitar skills.

"You should play guitar for us," she says.

You've thought of this. Her band is better than yours, but you could make their songs better with your guitar. You figure, without saying so, that the fact that the band is all women could be an issue. "I wish I could," you say.

"Seriously," Melissa says. "Some small labels and some A&R clowns are supposed to be at the Rat and I want us to sound our best." She smiles. "You play the main guitar parts and I can front the band and focus on my singing."

You feel enormously flattered.

"You'd have to dress in drag, though," she says.

You're drunk. Not seeing any potential repercussions. Plus, it's for Melissa. You shrug, say, "What the hell."

"You'd play a set with us in drag?"

"Why not?"

The band goes for the idea. The night of the show, Melissa shaves what little facial hair you have. She sits on your lap while she does your lips and eyes and cheeks. She tells you what a pretty girl you are. You feel yourself blush. She gives you a wig of hers, black with severely cut bangs like the rest of the Bell Jars.

For your outfit, she picks a short black dress with black stockings and a black girdle with garters for the stockings. Your cock starts to get hard when she's dressing you but if she notices it, she doesn't say anything. You're five foot eight and a hundred and thirty pounds. You remember thinking you were fat.

You've played a few practices with the band—dressed like yourself, thankfully—and the sound is good. They probably are one of the best bands in town, but you seem to make them even better. That night at the Rat, the show smokes. You feel weird, playing in heels, feeling the slip of the stockings in the shoes, the pull of the garters on the stockings, but it all seems to be going well and you have to admit, it's kind of sexy being all dressed up onstage next to Melissa, with whom you may or may not be madly in love.

After the show, you break down your gear and you have

to piss. You pause for a moment between the women's and the men's room, and you choose the men's room. You piss at a urinal—difficult around your girdle-style garter belt, but you make it. As you start to walk out of the men's room a huge skinhead punk looks down on you and says, "Faggot!" He punches you to the floor. The bathroom tiles are cold. You have passed out on these tiles before. The floor is covered with water and soap and piss and dirt and blood. You leave the wig there. You get up slowly, your nose bleeding.

That night, at Melissa's apartment, you are still dressed up while she gently puts ice on your broken nose. She buys more liquor than you would have needed on a normal night, but you are in pain. Your nose is broken. This is the fifth time—you know what a broken nose feels like and you have learned to fix them yourself in front of a mirror, which is what you do that night in her bathroom, your mascara raccooning around your eyes like Alice Cooper. After you straighten your nose, you nearly pass out. You start to wobble and you take off your heels. You can't breathe through the nose—it's too swollen to snort the blow that would numb the pain, but Melissa gives you her last three Percodans and she puts the ice on your nose and kisses your forehead several times, saying "My poor, poor, pretty baby" over and over.

There is talk, among the band, of having you join the Bell Jars. But then there's a review of the show in one of the city's most important underground zines:

Boston's The Bell Jars are the real thing, thanks mostly to frontwoman Melissa B's incredible charisma and vocals and her songs that bring to mind if Joni Mitchell rocked like Paul Westerberg. She's one-of-a-kind in a city of carbon-copy bands, and because of her, The Bell Jars may be Boston's NEXT BIG THING.

On the down side, it doesn't help this band that their best-looking chick is the dude who plays guitar in Junkyard.

This last line doesn't exactly smooth your way into the band. Melissa still wants you, but the rest of the band vetoes her. Talk of you joining the Bell Jars ends.

One night, holding hands in bed, listening to the rain outside and the Beatles on the stereo, you say, "I love you."

She snuggles closer to you. You have slept together almost every night for the last three months. There is a trust. A comfort you have never known. "I love you, too," she says.

"No," you say. "I mean I love you. Like in love."

Rain. Music quietly under the rain. You hear her take a couple of deep breaths. "You know who I am," she says. "What I am."

"I'm sorry," you say.

"Don't be sorry," she says. You are holding her but now she's turned away. "I love you more than I've loved anyone else. Can't that be enough?"

And you could say, no, that's not enough, because that's what you're feeling. But you feel like you've already stepped over some line. You lean your head into her shoulder blade. "That's enough," you say.

Not long after that, the Bell Jars break up and Melissa

decides to take off for Los Angeles. She asks you if you want to come, but you're scared. You'd only know one person in LA, and that person would, you're sure, be a star in a year or so. You're afraid of moving to a city you've never seen. A big city where you might be alone. And she doesn't love you—at least not the way you love her. So, you stay.

One of the last things you do before she goes is teach her the guitar part on the Beatles' "Her Majesty."

Around six months later—this is before the Internet, before cell phones and e-mail—someone says to you, "Did you hear what happened to Melissa?"

You haven't. You expect to learn she signed a major label deal.

And he tells you that she was raped and murdered in an alley after playing a show in LA, not long after moving there. You find out six months after it happened. You don't know any of the details and never will. Who did it. Where it happened. What exactly happened. You can't believe she's been gone six months and you had no idea.

There is no funeral you can go to. This will bother you forever.

You still can't hear the Beatles for too long without thinking of her. You have to leave the room whenever "Her Majesty" comes on.

You live your life in music. People ask you all the time: Beatles or Stones? Who would you rather listen to? You tell them, Stones—no contest—but you never really tell them why.

2

2012: You think the story about waking up in Montreal might be a lie that you told for so long that you now believe it's a fact. You know you blacked out and woke up miles away from where you were—probably not even the same state—that much you're positive about. You remember waking up on some guy's floor and taking the beer and leaving. You know that happened somewhere. But there are so many jumbled fragments and you don't trust yourself. There's a natural human desire to make sense out of any series of events. That doesn't mean, of course, that they *do* make sense.

But Canada seems like a stretch. Definitely one of those Vermont/New Hampshire–shaped states once. And you think it happened at least twice in different places. But for years, you were very fucked up. And for years, you also lied to people. Memories blur. Nabokov said that memory is a revision. Maybe you revised a lot of this wrong. You are honestly not sure.

2012–2013: You feel your brain getting worse. They told you this would happen with age. Your cycling is becoming more rapid than it's ever been. Although you've mentioned being "bipolar" to various people in your life, you have rarely given any details of your specific condition, instead relying on popular conceptions (and misconceptions) of the disorder, which do not usually include psychosis or the kind of frequency with which you swing between poles. There are two major types of bipolar. Along with the mixed, non-specified, cyclothymic (lower-grade) type, there's the most severe form, with the worst prognosis and highest risk of suicide: rapid cycling. The subcategory of rapid-rapid, or ultradian, cycling is the most unusual. This is what you have. While many with bipolar experience short bursts of ultradian cycling, you simply live there.

Technically, to be diagnosed with rapid-cycling bipolar, you need to have four manic episodes within a calendar year. But four episodes a year doesn't seem very rapid to you at all. In the year leading up to the release of your fourth novel you are firing off a few a month. Before they take you off the antidepressants that can complicate rapid cycling, you start having massive swings, sometimes within days or, on a few occasions, hours. You can feel amazing and in tune with the universe at noon but have absolutely no idea how you'll feel at six o'clock. You may want to kill yourself by then. You may desperately want to get loaded or drunk. You may still feel like your brain can process information ten times faster than normal, as though your fingers on a computer or a guitar cannot keep up with everything clicking into place in your brain. All you know is that, for you, even doubling the baseline minimum for standard rapid cycling would constitute what would be, at least recently, one of the least eventful years of your life.

But you are lucky in some ways. In a peak manic state, most people are paralyzed with the dilemma of choice—too many things racing around their mind but not slowing enough to be caught. But you can spend twenty-four hours mixing in a recording studio and feel like there are sparks coming out of your fingers you're so alive. You have written for seventy-two hours. Your focus, you find out, is rare for someone with your condition. Many people don't really function.

Still, while there are genetic components to becoming an addict, you—and everyone who has ever been in recovery—understand that there is still an element of choice involved. You can choose not to drink. You can choose not to take pills. You can work the steps and somehow make your way through life with more tools than you used to have to deal with shit. But increasingly—more than you have had to face since before you got clean—you are realizing the overwhelming truth that you can't *choose* not to be crazy. You take some of the strongest brain stabilizers available, but nothing's going to make it go away. In your case, even what it means to "control" it bears no resemblance to actual mood stability. People say that addicts are, at heart, control freaks. Using addicts know how they're going to feel in five minutes. Mental illness, on the other hand, is the ultimate loss of control.

Plus, when you're an addict who stopped, it's something of a redemption tale. And everybody loves one of those. When you have a mental illness that might only get worse, people don't really want to hear about that. The story arc of mental illness does not conform to the redemption tale.

More and more you are realizing that if you are ashamed of certain things you *did* when you drank and used drugs, you are ashamed of who you *are* with mental illness.

2002: You discover Schopenhauer is fabulous music to have playing when a woman uses a riding crop or a cane on your ass. You can't have music with lyrics. Tom Verlaine's *Warm and Cool* is great, too. Any Glenn Gould. *Mingus at Antibes.* Instrumentals are by far a superior soundtrack for this activity. Words can intrude when the body wants to take over. Lyrics make you think—music helps you just feel.

1981: Your dad's friend is visiting. He sleeps on your living-room floor and your mother clearly hates him. It's an awkward visit, as your dad is trying to talk his friend (who has just gotten divorced) into rehab. Your father's friend has served in Vietnam and done time in jail. He calls jail "the joint."

You are listening to Johnny Thunders and the Heartbreakers' *L.A.M.F.* Your dad is in the garage working on a car and you are alone at the kitchen table with his friend.

Your father's friend asks, "What is this fucking noise?" He has a gravelly deep voice that kind of scares you.

"It's punk," you say.

"Punk?" he says, smoking a hand-rolled cigarette. "This is punk?"

"Punk music," you say. "They're a punk band."

"Is your band a punk band?"

You say yes.

"In the joint a punk is someone who takes it up the ass." He laughs. "You take it up the ass, kid?"

The thought has never occurred to you. You're fifteen, a slow developer. You've barely done more than make out with anyone. But you pick up on what he thinks the right answer is: "No."

"Then don't go calling yourself a punk. Punks take it up the ass. You tell the wrong person you're a punk and you'll be getting fucked in the ass, understand me, kid?"

Your dad walks in during his friend's last sentence. "What are you talking to my kid about?"

The friend shrugs. "Some life advice." He winks at you.

Years later, another band of yours plays a bar called the Joint. That night is also the first night a woman ever fucks you with a strap-on. She is the bartender at the Joint, and she drives you to her place while the band shares a room at some shit motel near the highway. She wears a vintage dress, fishnets, and Chuck Taylors, none of which she has taken off, while you are naked in front of her.

Just as she starts to fuck you, you remember what your father's friend said. You think of having met this woman in the Joint and that you are in a band that gets labeled in the press as "Cow-Punk." You are a punk and you hear that gravelly voice say, "A punk is someone who takes it up the ass, kid." You think of all these things and you start to laugh.

The bartender stops for a moment. "Are you okay?"

You are drunk. You try to stop laughing because it seems inappropriate at the moment. "I'm fine," you say, still try-ing to stop laughing. "Sorry."

1973: For show-and-tell in the third grade, you bring in your father's copy of Redd Foxx's *You Gotta Wash Your Ass.* You lip-synch to his performance. You get suspended.

The next week, you bring Tom Waits's *Small Change,* which has a stripper with pasties on the album cover. You are suspended again.

Your favorite song this year is "Everybody's Talkin'" from the *Midnight Cowboy* soundtrack. So you go to the pub-lic library and read about the movie. You like the name of one of the movie's characters. Ratso Rizzo. There is a pic-ture of Dustin Hoffman as Ratso. He looks cool.

For the third-grade Halloween costume party, you dress as Ratso Rizzo. You slick your hair back with soap and your father's VO5. You wear your raincoat with nothing on underneath—you take your clothes off in the bathroom. You walk around, hitting other students' desks, the walls, the lockers, screaming "I'm walkin' here!" in your best ap-proximation of a Ratso Rizzo voice. You've only read about the scene, so you have no idea what Ratso really sounds like.

When the principal asks you why you're naked under the coat, you say you thought that's how perverts dressed.

He shakes his head. "Perverts?" he says. "A pervert costume?" He's still shaking his head as he dials what you assume is your parents' phone number.

FEBRUARY 27, 2006: Your wife, Gayle, wakes up in extreme pain. The band you're in together, the Danbury Shakes, had played a show earlier and her shoulders were too sore to carry her bass cabinet. This is unusual. Gayle spends three hours at the gym every day. She's cut and ripped and takes tremendous pride in her body. Exercise is the way she blows off steam from a stressful day of grading papers.

You met Gayle in grad school in 1989. You moved in together in 1993 when she was getting her PhD in French feminism. You'd never met someone that put together. Someone able to read Derrida and Lacan and Irigaray and make heads or tails of them. You are stunned. You, who bounced through five states and three graduate programs, having someone so well-adjusted and smart and high-functioning and ambitious fall in love with you. In her thirties, just for fun, Gayle takes up the bass, so you guys can have a band together. She gets everything done she ever sets her mind to.

That night, after the show, she wakes up with her entire body in debilitating pain. Her legs and feet are cramping. She says, "It's like my body's betraying me."

The pain has been building, but not for that long. When

she tiled the bathroom you were restoring during winter break, her hands grew fatigued and sore after only a few hours of work.

Now her pain seems excruciating. You desperately want to fix whatever is wrong with her. You wish it could be you suffering instead.

This leads to the Year of Doctors. Diagnosis after diagnosis, treatment after treatment. When nothing Western works, she tries acupuncture; she tries every Eastern-medicine quack she can find. Nothing seems to help. Eventually, she gets so exhausted from seeking treatments, she sees a pain doctor who puts her on OxyContin for the daily pain and Vicodin for the breakthrough pain. You don't think much about it. You've had liquor in the house for fifteen years since you cleaned up and never been tempted to touch it. It's simply part of your past—nothing more or less. That's just not you anymore.

2007: Gayle's diagnoses continue to mount. Doctor after doctor calls her a medical mystery. One thinks she has fibromyalgia. Another mentions something the medical community is calling a newly discovered form of MS. The only good news is that these are non-degenerative. She's also battling chronic fatigue syndrome, which you quickly realize should have a more serious name. She can spend more than a week in bed, unable to read or do anything, and not get restorative sleep. They have no idea how any of these illnesses started but suspect the chronic fatigue was as a result of a virus that attacked her stomach, maybe years earlier, and then eventually shot her immune system to hell.

Another doctor says she doesn't believe in fibromyalgia. Out in the parking lot, Gayle says to you, "Well, if she doesn't believe in it, what the fuck is wrong with me?"

You don't know what to say.

She says, "*Something* is very fucking wrong with me."

You say yes, something is clearly wrong, and you both curse the doctor who just treated her like shit.

"If a fucking *man* walked in there," she asks, "would some doctor tell him it was all in his head?"

With her meds, Gayle can grit her way through the pain. But there's no way to fight total exhaustion. For the first time in her life, she calls in sick to work. Many people with her conditions go on permanent disability. Some kill themselves.

You stop making plans with friends for dinner because there's no way she can know how she'll feel on any given day. You stop seeing plays because it's impossible to know if she will have the energy to make it anywhere on time, or even if she can make it out the door. You begin to have sex far less often. Your life grows smaller by degrees. Soon you are too exhausted to even think about sex, no matter how Gayle feels about it.

You have no idea what to do.

After Gayle's pain begins, you massage her for at least an hour most nights, trying to alleviate her terrible pain. But nothing works. And you are doing nothing but brooding and falling apart. After a year of this, you start to withdraw. You are reminded of Hemingway's line about how you go bankrupt—slowly at first, and then all of a sudden. It builds, and then you break. You turn inward. You are ignoring friends and not returning e-mails or phone calls. It is less than six months before you relapse. Your shrink, who you start seeing when thoughts of suicide get more intense, tells you to be careful of "caregiver fatigue," something you have never heard of.

There is a saying in AA and NA: *You go out before you ever go out.* You don't think this will happen to you. You are just exhausted. That's all it is.

MID-1970S: Every Sunday, you have to visit your mother's parents. You don't like them. You don't particularly *hate* them, though your dad does seem to actively dislike them. But, then, they hate him and treat him like shit, so you can kind of see where he's coming from. Both of your parents do nothing but complain about them.

But, even though you don't hate them, you still have no interest in wasting your Sundays when you could be with your friends, or playing basketball, or simply be alone. Plus, every week you have to eat something known as "Great-Grandma Mary's Meat Recipe," which makes everyone ill. The whole family either has to crap or puke halfway home. Plus, their house is a mess. As a kid, you will only think it's messy, but over the years you'll see that it is more than messy. Your grandmother never throws anything away. Even in the '70s, there's a basement filled with so much stuff, you can't walk around—it's just a pile of furniture and clothing and huge garbage bags swollen and piled all over one another. The attic is impossible to get into.

Your grandparents are the only people you know of who have a party line for a phone. You find this otherworldly. You pick up their phone, and any one of their neighbors might be using it. About the only fun you and your sister have at their house is picking up the receiver as gently as possible, hoping to hear a voice instead of a dial tone. When you do hear a voice, it's usually pretty mundane—you will remember a woman talking about slippage in her dentures—but at least it's more entertaining than what's happening in the house.

One Sunday, you get to their house and the screen door is unlocked and you see your grandmother rolling cigarettes in the kitchen. She's using her brown rolling machine, the one you kind of love. Some of your best memories with her are rolling her cigarettes while she drinks, her smeared lipstick staining her whiskey glass as her speech slowly becomes more slurred. After she passes out in her chair, you take sips from her glass. The whiskey is strong, but the more disgusting part is the lipstick residue, which tastes like a greasy pair of wax lips.

What's weird today is the band of gauze wrapped around her head, bloodied on one temple so she looks like the fife player in the *Spirit of '76* painting. She's staring straight ahead blankly, as if she doesn't notice that the four of you have come into the kitchen.

Your mother says, "Mom! What happened?"

Your grandmother is clearly drunk—pretty early in the day, even for her. She slurs, "Your father shot me."

"What?"

Your grandmother doesn't seem that upset. Maybe dazed, but not angry. "Your father shot me, dear."

Your father says, "Shot you?"

It's the first time you've ever heard your grandmother say "dear." It's about the most cordial she's ever sounded.

You and your sister look at each other, confused.

"Where the hell is Bob?" your father asks, referring to your grandfather.

Your grandmother never interrupts her cigarette rolling, except to take another sip of her drink or a drag of her smoke. "Outside." She pauses. "Be careful, dear. He has a gun."

Eventually your grandfather walks into the kitchen with his .22-caliber rifle. "I didn't hear you pull up."

Your mother turns around and points at the rifle. "Is that loaded?"

"Of course it's loaded. It's hard to shoot if it's not."

"You shot Mom?"

"I was outside," he says.

"What the fuck does that matter?"

Your grandmother says, in a flat emotionless slur, "You're in front of the children."

Your mother takes a deep breath and looks at her mother. "And your husband has a loaded *gun* in front of my children."

Your father says, "Could you put the gun in the barn, Bob?"

"Why is everybody treating me like I don't know how to use a gun?"

Your mother says, "It looks like you know how to use a gun pretty well, Dad."

"I was out shooting gophers," he says. "One shot ricocheted off a rock and came into the house."

"And hit Mom!" your mother says.

You are a little confused, because your mother can't seem to stand her mother. It will take you many more years to realize that relationships between parents and children can be complex enough that you can not want to see them, you might even fear or hate them, but you will still not want them dead.

Your father orders you and your sister into the living room, where the big stone fireplace is, but you can still hear all the yelling from the kitchen.

Your mother says, "Do you need a hospital?"

Your grandfather says, "Oh, Jesus Christ. It was an accident."

"She could still need a hospital, Bob," your father says.

"It grazed her," he says. "Plus, then I'd have to explain that I didn't shoot her."

Your mother says, "You *did* shoot her!"

"I shot her," your grandfather says. "But I didn't *shoot* her!"

You don't remember much more about that day, except for your father going outside and walking around, and then later looking at the hole in the window from the bullet.

On the way home, your father says to your mother, "There's no way that bullet could have come from him shooting in the garden."

Your father's not a ballistics expert, but he is in law enforcement. You believe him on that drive home. You believe him now.

1995: Driving cross-country from visiting her family in California, you and Gayle decide on a whim to get married in Las Vegas. You didn't plan this. But you didn't plan on moving in together either, and that's been going great for two years, so it seems like something fun to do. Gayle's always been against the institution of marriage. You've never cared one way or the other—though you did once ask Mary to marry you, but you did that when you were desperate not to lose her and it seemed only some grand gesture would prevent that. But with Gayle, somewhere between Southern California and Las Vegas, getting married goes from being a joke to an idea to a plan.

When you get to Vegas, though, all the hotels are full except for one that's having some labor dispute. The workers picket out front, protesting their wages.

"That's a bad sign," Gayle says.

"How so?"

"I don't want some scab wedding," she says, and you fall in love just a little more.

You end up getting married in Salt Lake City. It takes all of an hour. You ask the lady doing it to leave out god, but she still asks if you will marry Gayle in front of god and all these witnesses.

You pause. "Okay."

The lady looks at you sternly.

"I do," you say.

Then she gives you a list of about twenty things, including your soul, that you are promising Gayle for the rest of your lives. When she turns to Gayle, she only asks if Gayle will cherish you. Gayle waits for the rest of her list and, finally realizing there's nothing more coming, she says yes.

When you are walking out of the building, you turn to her and jokingly say, "I better feel cherished."

1972: You watch some animated PBS children's special about protecting the environment. They try to get kids to care by focusing on the extinction of various species. They focus on one called the Newfoundland wolf, which went extinct in 1911. Your grandmother lived in a world that had this wolf, and now it's gone forever. For some reason this devastates you. This is your earliest memory of being too upset to eat. You sit at the dinner table, thinking about the last Newfoundland wolf, still alive but without any hope. You wonder if it was capable of feeling how alone it was in the world.

"What's wrong?" your father says. "Why aren't you eating?"

But you are afraid to talk. Afraid that if you even open your mouth, you'll start crying, and you know that you are not supposed to cry, so you just move your food around and try to disappear.

You become obsessed with extinct animals. You spend all your time thinking about what it would be like to be the last of your kind. First, as one of the last two of your kind, and then just alone, waiting to die. You think of the most alone you have ever felt and realize it can always be worse. There are types of alone you can only imagine until they happen.

You make lists of all the extinct animals you care about in your notebooks. You do several show-and-tells in a row where you present reports about the Catahoula salamander (date of extinction, 1964), the Tacoma pocket gopher (1970), the Cuban red macaw (1860s), and the passenger pigeon (1914).

Your teacher sends you home with a note that you figure out from overhearing your parents is about how your obsession with death is disturbing the other students. But she's wrong. You are not obsessed with death. You are obsessed by the fear of being alone.

1992: Your friend Linda comes from New York, where she's now living, to visit you at your dead grandmother's farmhouse in Connecticut, which you are cleaning out in exchange for living there. Linda was one of your roommates in Boston when you lived in Southie—the one who used to joke that if it weren't for you, she never would have met every pierced and tattooed slutty bartender in Boston at her breakfast table.

You are making Linda dinner. Your grandmother's hoarder house is still pretty disgusting, even though you have been living there for months and have already cleaned out what would be seven or eight lifetimes' worth of shit in any ordinary house. Here, though, this has done little more than create actual walkways between rooms and some empty spots on the furniture so that you can sit down. By this point, there aren't rodent carcasses littering the floors anymore, but it smells like there are still some around, hidden under the remaining junk. Linda manages million-dollar apartments in New York. She has actually flown first class. You can hardly believe she is even willing to set foot in this disaster, much less eat and sleep here, so you are trying to make it as nice for her as possible. You go grocery shopping together, buying things you know she likes, and when it comes time to check out, you pay like a host is supposed to, writing the third check you have ever written in your life.

You are twenty-six years old. This is your first checking account. You ask Linda what the date is.

"The eighteenth," she says.

You stand there holding the pen. "What month?"

She looks at you incredulously. "Wow. What I'd give to live in your weird little world," she says.

You've been a drunk the whole time you've known Linda, but you haven't seen her in a while, and your addiction has progressed more than you want to admit to yourself. You are calling yourself a writer, but the truth is you have written three pages in six months. You drink until you pass out every night and you paint houses and factories as your main job. Your second job is one night a week at a microbrewery where you work the bottling line. Every twelfth bottle is what's known as a "short"—it only fills up eleven instead of twelve ounces—and so you get to take home four cases of eleven-ounce beers every Thursday night. You tell yourself you will never run out of beer, but you are frequently out by Sunday afternoon.

Although you and Linda were always platonic in Boston, alone in the hoarder house, you end up sleeping together. Before you get very far, Linda takes a deep breath and says, "I promised myself if I did this, I'd really *do* it." Her voice is more shy than you've ever heard it. "Would you tie me up and spank me?" She's the first woman who's ever asked you to do this. You say, "Of course," because she asked, which you know took nerve, even if it isn't the sort of thing you fantasize about. It isn't that you don't enjoy it—you've always thought Linda was beautiful, and you're turned on by the chance to make her happy, but also, privately, as you belt her pale ass, watching the welts rise, you're really imagining that it's you tied up and she is using the belt on you.

Later, when Linda's hands are untied and you're holding each other, she says, "Thank you. I was so afraid to ask for that." And you will feel a moment briefly opening—the opportunity to be as brave as she was and ask if she will do the same thing to you. But instead you just hold her, you can't find the words, and the moment passes, and soon she is heading back to New York, and you never ask.

1997: Gayle gets the news that she's had an irregular Pap smear. You go with her to the gynecologist and he tells her that he doesn't like what he sees. He says it's no big deal and in a calm voice says he wants to do surgery the next morning.

"Tomorrow?" Gayle says.

You don't know what to say. You sit up in your chair and lean toward his desk like you're going to ask a question, but you can't speak. The room spins.

The doctor says, "I don't want you to sit around worrying. It's best for everyone if we do this right off." He's a white guy from South Africa, and you will always remember his accent when he says "right off" instead of "right away."

He tells you both that it's not cancer but something called carcinoma in situ—something that will lead to cancer if left untreated. He shows you diagrams and pictures while you're in his office. All of this is almost impossible to follow. His voice sounds like it's underwater.

You say, "How serious is this?"

"Again," he says, "it's nothing we can't take care of. And we'll do that right off."

You and Gayle spend most of the car ride to see her parents reassuring each other. Repeating what he said about it not being a big deal—just something that needs to be taken care of. She seems calmer than you are. You want to scream. Or run. You feel trapped in the car as she drives. You crack the window and wish you still smoked, but you quit together earlier in the year.

You are broke, and her parents offer to pay for the surgery. You don't like your father-in-law—he's the angriest drunk you have ever met—but you are enormously grateful and feel guilty for how much you complain about him.

You don't sleep that night. The next morning, when they are getting ready to wheel Gayle into surgery, you hold her hand while the nurses sedate her, only letting go when they bring in yet another piece of paper for her to sign. More nurses come in. The anesthesiologist. Finally, the surgeon. He tells you both again how this isn't anything to worry about. It's not a major procedure. She'll be in and out in a couple of hours.

You tell Gayle you love her as they wheel her into the operating room. She's nodding in and out from the drugs but tells you she loves you, too. She tells you she'll be fine, though she looks a little scared, and you remember thinking that you are the one who's supposed to be comforting her, not the other way around.

Two hours pass. Three. Four. And you start to think something has gone terribly wrong. Sitting helpless in the waiting room, you think about Gayle dying. You feel guilty for even thinking this, but you can't help it. You think about losing her. About being alone again. You don't think you can live without her. The minutes tick by slower. You calmly decide that you will kill yourself if she doesn't make it through this—the surgery or after it. Losing Gayle feels like it would be losing everything, and you don't want to face the world again without her.

2013: You are afraid of losing your mind.

You write yourself notes, lists:

- Pugilistic dementia (CTE)
- Worsening bipolar
- Post-concussive syndrome

- Frontal lobe . . . impulse control and decision making
- Dr. says there's no cure.
- MRIs inconclusive. May have the early signs. They don't know if or when it will get worse.
- Eventually, might forget how to get home. Won't be able to drive. Will have to be watched at all times. Won't have the luxury of being alone again. Can't imagine anything that could make you feel *more* alone.
- Everybody's entire existence will be determined by watching you to make sure you're safe.
- Can live like this as it is now.
- Can't live if this gets worse.

1982: Mary—who seven years from now will be your fiancée—is absolutely in love with R.E.M. You go to high school together, though she's two years behind you. You are just close friends at this point—she's dating some college guy from out of town who you hate. Her best friend is dating one of your best friends. You are always together.

She plays R.E.M. for you every chance she gets. You are not nearly as taken with them as she is, and one night you are drinking beer on her father's porch and you tell her that you like certain parts of a lot of their songs but never the whole song, it seems. You will later end up loving some of their songs, but that's how you feel at the time.

You specifically mention "Radio Free Europe." The verses are dull and unmemorable, but the chorus is amazing. Their songs just never seem to be great all the way through—there's always something that doesn't work.

"But don't you get it?" she says. "It's the bad parts that make you realize how good the great parts are."

You will live many more years. Many more, in fact, than anyone would have predicted for you. You will read—and sometimes even understand—Nietzsche and Heidegger and Aristotle and Confucius and a bunch of other great thinkers, trying to make some sense out of your world. But you often think that you have never heard a better philosophy than what Mary says that night, drunk on her back porch: It's the bad parts that make you realize how good the great parts are.

3

1995: The night you and Gayle get married while driving cross-country, you stay in what passes for a posh hotel in Salt Lake City.

You stay on the eleventh floor—the highest up you have ever slept in your life.

In bed, you ask her why she has two pillows and you have one.

"Because they only gave us three," she says.

And you know you are in love.

SEPTEMBER 1, 1914: Martha, the last known passenger pigeon in the world, dies at the Cincinnati Zoo. The cause is old age, and Martha has spent her last four years as the last of her kind. Various estimates put her age at anywhere from seventeen to twenty-nine, with twenty-nine being the consensus.

2009: You've relapsed for a year, after nearly fifteen years clean. After your relapse, after you decide not to kill yourself, you start over with AA. You go through the dreadful shame of taking a newcomer chip. You try to be humble about it. You try to make ninety meetings in ninety days like you're supposed to. You follow all of your new sponsor's directions. You make gratitude lists. You do affirmations— your sponsor tells you to list good qualities you have, even if you haven't always lived up to them. You wince when you write things like:

- Good friend
- Kind
- Smart
- Funny
- Reliable (?)
- Can be honest. Have *been* honest

Some days you get stuck after two or three items and you have to check what you wrote the day before to see what good qualities you might have, or have had.

You admit you are powerless in the face of your addiction and you need help. You try hard to admit you're no better or smarter than anyone else there, though you cringe every time someone mentions their religion and thanks "Jesus Christ as my lord and savior." Your friend Patrick, who's been to San Quentin and turned his life around totally and is the person whose recovery you respect most, tells you to just do the steps.

"The program is harder for smart people and skeptics," he says. "Stick with it, bro."

You listen. You have no choices left.

2010: A year after quitting opiates a second time, you slowly teach yourself to write again. At first, you can barely write a sentence.

The last two years are something that would kill you to repeat. You're not as fragile as people think. But you know your limits.

One night you delete all your suicide notes from your computer.

If things go bad again, it's not like you can't write a new one.

1996: Nine-year-old Amber Hagerman is abducted. Four days later, her body is found, throat slit. Her murder inspires the AMBER Alert System. The case remains unsolved.

JULY 1977: One night, at sunset, you sit against the outside wall of your garage and chain-smoke some cigarettes you've stolen from your father. Nicole has been dead less than a month. The cigarettes make your throat raw, and you love it. Anything that makes you feel different than the way you normally feel is always welcome. You're spending hours with a sharp piece of gravel, rubbing off the skin on the back of your left hand until it wells with blood from the deep abrasion. The air lets out of your chest and you feel a tension leave your body.

It will not leave a tremendous scar, but you will be able to see it for the rest of your life. You watch the sun set, smoking your father's cigarettes as you draw your own blood and start to breathe easier.

Pain becomes one of the most complicated things in your life. Some pain that comes at you in waves feels like it can destroy you. Emotional pain from outside, especially from men, makes you feel weak and small and never good enough. Pain you inflict on yourself—and later, pain inflicted by women who care about you—is calming and settling. You learn early that pain is as complex and wide-ranging as love itself.

1984: You are having sex with Donna, your friend's mother.

For years, when you tell this story, you'll say you lost your virginity to your friend's mom—which, while it is the emotional truth, only echoes the factual truth. But *I lost my virginity to my friend's mom* is a good shorthand for how you spent your senior year.

You and Donna have a secret affair for more than six months. You make out like kids, hiding behind corners of buildings and hoping no one sees. She kisses aggressively, sucking your tongue with a force that makes you feel she could tear it out and swallow it. She's the first woman to bite your nipples. The first to intentionally make you feel pain and you float with the realization that you love it. Someone else hurting you feels better—even more calming—than when you hurt yourself.

You meet her at commuter train station parking lots and she looks over her shoulder every time a car pulls in. Her mouth tastes like Virginia Slims and Tab when you meet her after work, and like Virginia Slims and some bitter white wine later in the day. She teaches you where to touch her and how to go down on her in her bedroom after she and her husband have separated and you are, on occasion, alone in her house. Even though she is the first woman you make orgasm, you will never actually *have* an orgasm with her. The closest you get is once when the two of you are alone in the house on a Saturday and she is giving you your first blow job in the upstairs hallway when the garage door starts to open. Your friend has come home when he'd said he'd be gone all day. You have just closed your eyes and felt lips and a tongue and teeth on your cock for the first time. You have never felt this good without being loaded. It may be even slightly better than being loaded. When she hears the garage door, Donna stops going down on you and rushes into the bathroom as you zip up your pants and wonder what room you should race to be in when your friend gets upstairs. Standing in the hallway with an obvious hard-on seems the wrong place to be. You hurry toward the kitchen and you hear Donna brushing her teeth in the bathroom. She never goes down on you again.

You love your friend and feel terribly guilty about being with his mother. You also despise him for coming home in the middle of your first blow job. You could, you real-

ize, punch him. You're an emotional mess. You're in love
with a woman twice your age and you are such a rube, you
think that you will be together forever. You wonder how
it's going to work when your friend is your stepson. You actually try to get your head around this and more troubling
situations. You are mugged by guilt every day. Your friend
is the person you would tell about this if it was anyone else's
mother. Instead, you have no one to talk to and you realize
for the first time that being in love is not something that
makes everything all right. Sometimes everything that's
wonderful with her is shadowed with a cold feeling that
you are, on some foundational level, a bad person.

You love—or at least think you love—Donna. But that
doesn't stop you from drinking her liquor and stealing pills
out of her medicine cabinet. She takes a lot of Valium. Now
you take a lot of Valium. She has Percocet and you promise
yourself you won't take enough for her to notice, but you
go through her whole script in a week. If she notices, she
doesn't say anything. You fall asleep a lot at school. The
assistant principal takes you into his office and talks about
potential that you're not living up to, and he tells you that
you're selling the sizzle and not the steak and that he needs
to see more steak and less sizzle out of you and you are
loaded and you wonder what the fuck he is talking about.

One night, Donna takes you to a cemetery two towns
over. She doesn't talk in the car—doesn't even kiss you
when you get in. She stares straight ahead and you count
four Virginia Slims with coral lipstick on their filters piled
in the ashtray by the time she parks.

She starts up a hill and then waits for you. She takes your hand when you get to her and she starts walking uphill again. You will still feel bad about this years later, feel awful that you are so clueless as to miss how serious she is, but climbing that hill the only thought in your head is that you are getting fucked in a cemetery. Great plan. Who would find you there?

She takes her hand out of yours and lights a cigarette. You feel nervous and unsure of what to do, and you light one as well.

You are standing in between some headstones and she points to the one next to you.

"That's my sister," she says.

It becomes clear you are almost certainly *not* going to fuck in this cemetery. That doesn't seem to matter because she brought *you* here. Not anyone else. That has to mean something. But you have no idea what to say.

You manage, "I'm sorry." Your friend has told you about the aunt he barely remembers who died in a car accident.

You both stand there for a while. She tells you that you are not allowed to tell anyone what she's about to tell you.

"I just need someone to hear this, okay?"

"Of course," you say.

She tells you there was no car accident. Their mother found her hanging in the basement ten years ago. You think of your friend's doting grandmother. You never would have guessed that she'd dealt with shit this major. But she's sixty-five years old. Of course she has—everyone does.

Donna says, very calmly, "She killed herself." As she

walks down the hill, you look at the dates on the headstone and do some quick math—she wasn't even thirty years old. You follow Donna back to her car.

You get in and she starts driving. She says, "You know you are the only person in ten years who has heard any-thing about what really happened to her?"

Again—what are you supposed to say? The tires thump over construction gates and potholes and you pass the giant quarry on the right where you used to swim in the summer until some kid got run over and killed walking home from a party. After that the cops chained it off.

"Why?" you say. You're not even sure now what you meant—was it: *Why are you telling me this?* Or, *Why lie about it?* Or, *Why did she do it?*

She says, "Because, she was in a car accident." She smiles and shakes her head. "Ask my fucking mother. Car acci-dent." She tosses her cigarette out the window and lights another one with the car's cigarette plug. When she's done, you push the lighter back in and light one of your own, feeling the warmth from the heat coils as you breathe in.

She says, "Apparently, if you pretend something didn't happen, then it didn't happen."

Things between you get more complicated over the course of your senior year. To stave off suspicion, Donna tells you that you should probably have a girlfriend your own age. You don't want a girlfriend. You love Donna. This *must* be what love feels like, though you are not able to say the words to her for fear of what her response might be.

You end up dating Kris. Now you feel, if possible,

worse. You don't love Kris. After two weeks together you realize you don't even particularly *like* her. But you feel really awful because she's just some pawn in this increasingly complex and fucked-up life of yours.

When you start going out, there seems to be some unwritten rule that says a boyfriend drives the girlfriend to school. No one told you about this rule. The first few days, she sings along with some hideous shit like Journey or Starship on the radio. This starts to drive you insane, because she sings off-key and doesn't know a lot of the words. You start making sure there are tapes playing by the time you pick her up—maybe she only sings along to stuff she knows from the radio. You try Bob Dylan. Lou Reed. Jonathan Richman. Marianne Faithfull. She sings along to all of it, though she doesn't know a single word to any of them. The next week, you are about to snap, so you play instrumental music—tapes by the Mahavishnu Orchestra. The Glenn Phillips Band. An experimental Glenn Branca piece you don't even like that sounds like wrecking balls and arc welding and the cries of dying animals.

She sings along to all of it.

After school, you sit at the kitchen table with Donna and your friend. Your friend asks you about the prom. You say you guess you'll be taking Kris. Donna gets a dark frown and takes her glass of wine and goes to her bedroom, slamming the door. You want to follow her and ask what's wrong, but you can't. You and your friend stay at the table.

Later, when you and Donna end up alone in the laundry room, you ask her if you did something.

She seems angry at you for the first time. "I don't need to hear about you and your fucking *girlfriend*," she says.

"She was your idea."

"Just go," she says, waving you away with a cigarette between her lips. "Go. Go fuck your little girl with her tight little ass and her perky tits, okay?"

You stand there. You have no idea what's happening.

"Go!"

You leave.

She stops talking to you for ten days. You feel weak with the fear that you're losing her. That she doesn't like you anymore.

One day, you are hanging out at the house and the phone rings. You often hang after school at their house, so you don't have to go to your own. Donna is at work, and your friend is out picking up something to drink. You figure you'll take a message.

You say hello and a woman who mistakes you for your friend—she calls you by his name—starts talking. "Your mother is a whore, do you know that?"

"What?"

She uses your friend's name again. "Listen to me. She's fucking Harry and god knows who else that slut spreads her legs for. Your mother is a filthy whore."

You hang up. *Harry?* Harry is a guy she works with. He has a '70s porn mustache and a horseshoe balding pattern and he wears brown suits with ridiculously wide ties. The phone rings and you stupidly answer it and the woman is back, her voice a droning menace telling you your mother is a whore, your mother is a whore, your mother is a whore, and you hang up again. The next time it rings, you don't answer.

By June, Donna totally avoids you. You get the message and stop going to her house. Which means you are stuck at yours. You feel terrible about Kris and break up with her. You are mildly relieved when she doesn't seem to care much and is quickly dating some other guy and no doubt singing along to whatever the fuck music plays in his pickup truck every morning.

1988: It takes you four years to get the courage to go back to Donna's house. To try to set things right. It was a fucked-up relationship, but you are beginning to see that just about everyone you know is a royal mess. Why should she have been an exception just because she was twice your age? You are still feeling guilty about the whole thing—that your friend, to the best of your knowledge, has never known about any of this.

You call first and ask if she's alone and if you can come over and she quietly says yes to both questions, after considering them for an uncomfortably long time.

It's freezing. You knock and it's so cold your knuckles hurt from rapping on the door. After a minute or so, she opens it, but blocks your entrance to the house.

She sounds young—more than you ever would have remembered—when she says a quiet, shy-sounding "Hi."

"Hey," you say. "Can I come in?"

She looks down and seems to step out of the way. You open the screen door and it catches on your sweater. You'd hoped to play this like an older, more mature version of you who could sit with Donna and you could talk like two adults and have this end on the right note. Instead, you are an idiot stuck in her door.

While you are cursing her screen, she turns around. She looks at you—and it will bother you forever, even though you know it does not matter, that the last time she sees you, you are tangled in her screen door. So much for the older, more mature you. You feel like you might break down on the porch and you look away from her eyes because you think you're crying.

She says, "I can't talk to you," and closes the door. You are still awkwardly stuck in her screen door as you hear her walk upstairs toward what you know is her bedroom. The lights go out, including the porch light. You finally pull yourself free from the fucking screen and you start to walk away, realizing that you've been cut from her story. Now you didn't happen, either.

2013: You are telling this story of Donna from such a distance. You've told it to close friends. You have altered it over time, to make it more effective. To try to have it resonate with your friends the ways it did and does with you. You've changed it around so much, you can't remember how it really happened. But what you're telling now, this story about being stuck in Donna's screen door, is— no matter how much you may have altered the timing or chronology—the truest version of the story you will ever know.

4

1971: You parents are fighting. They're in their bedroom, but you can always hear them fight, partially because they yell, partially because your father hangs his dry cleaning over their bedroom door so that it never fully closes. They usually fight about money. You are young, but you know that much.

This fight, though, seems to be about you. It will take you many years to realize it was about *them*, but that's not how you understood it.

Your mother says something about how much trouble you are. How hard you are to handle.

You father says, "Do you think I wanted kids in the first place?"

Your mother, at least for the moment, stops arguing.

1988: Chet Baker, trumpet player and singer, dies from a fall from an Amsterdam balcony while under the influence of cocaine and heroin.

SEPTEMBER 1993: You have a second seizure a couple of days after your first, not long after you quit drinking. It's not as bad as the first one, but still harrowing enough to have you curled in a fetal position for hours after you regain consciousness. You spend six hours staring at the far corner of your bedroom, staring at the shadows of the leaves on the far wall. You don't remember those six hours elapsing—you only know it is six hours because you keep a notebook by the bed. You keep checking the digital clock in between staring at the wall and make lines like in the old prison movies, one line for every five minutes, in groups of four vertical and one diagonal. You later count fourteen of the five-line sections and four more vertical lines, so technically it's six hours and ten minutes. In between several of the five-lined sections, you have written the word "no" more than fifty times.

This is a lie you will tell people for years—the last bit about the "noes." You actually find thirty-one and only about twenty of them are perfectly legible. The rest you can't actually read and just assume are "no" since that's what all the other ones say.

Your head feels like you've banged it against a wall repeatedly. The back of your skull is tender to the touch. Your tongue tastes like coins. You remember very little of what happens after your seizures. You have no idea when they will stop, or if they will stop. You live in deep fear of what you have done to yourself.

After six hours and ten minutes, you have no idea what you do. There is nothing else in the notebook and no memory of the time that passes.

1990: You and Mary are on vacation on the east coast of Mexico in some small town whose name you will forget. You spend the night at a bar with some expats and Mary tries to get you to dance, but as always you refuse, too embarrassed to dance in front of anyone. She dances with some drunk guy who comes on to her and she laughingly brushes him off.

Later, while you are in bed at a run-down, adorable hotel, you hold each other while the rain starts. Slowly at first, but soon it becomes a storm. You are both drunk, in great moods, and you fuck to the sound of the rain battering the roof tiles.

In the morning, you tell her that you'll go find some coffee and bring it to her, but you can't find anyone in the hotel. The entire first floor is under at least six inches of water, and there's no one to be found at the front desk. You go back upstairs and the two of you head into town looking for coffee. You are hungover, too, and think about having a beer to calm your nerves and get rid of your headache.

The town is flooded and deserted. It's a warm, beautiful morning—about eighty degrees with a gentle breeze and you feel the sun on your face and Mary's hand in yours and you start to walk around the town square. There is so much water that you can't tell when you're on the sidewalk or in the street until you take a step and your foot sinks another six inches. Then you are up to your knees until you find your way back to the sidewalk.

The whole town is like a scene from *On the Beach*. It's like someone dropped a bomb that left the buildings standing and took away all the people.

Over an hour later, you will finally find a café that's open and the owners will tell you that there was a hurricane the night before. That you have been out walking in the eye of the storm, and you need to stay with them while the hurricane passes through again.

But for now, you are alone, together, holding hands and in love and feeling like the last people on earth on a beautiful day. You will remember thinking it's impossible to be as happy as you are with Mary, but you are. The two of you wander the abandoned, flooded town square. Palm trees, almost naked from losing their fronds in the storm, quietly sway above you in front of a brilliantly blue cloudless sky.

2012: Junior Seau, an All-Pro football player with CTE, kills himself. Gunshot to the chest. You add him to your list of people with CTE and people who kill themselves.

1985–1993: You get bills from hospitals a few times a year. You have no idea why you were in these hospitals. Sometimes a friend knows. Sometimes you ask a roommate and they look at you and say, "You don't *know* if you were in a *hospital?*"

"Well, I think I must have been," you say.

And you must have been. But you don't remember why. And after the first bill, you don't try to find out why, because trying to find out means talking to the very people to whom you owe tremendous amounts of money. Money you don't have. Money you think may exceed your life's earnings when everything's tallied up and you shift tense.

You will tell lies to explain it. Part of this is because you don't know what happened. But you also like a good story. Mostly you worry that the world hates you as much as you hate yourself and you had better invent a character who's more interesting than you. It's the only way you expect anyone to want to stick around for long—convincing them that you are someone you are not. You don't lie, like some people, out of any desire to make money or get ahead materially—you lie, like some other people, because you are very afraid of being alone. Of anyone knowing the truth. If no one ever really knows who you are, you—the real you—can never be rejected.

1955: The novelist Gabriel García Márquez is working as a journalist for a newspaper in Bogotá. In February, he covers a shipwreck off the coast of Alabama, in the Gulf of Mexico. Several crew members drown. One crew member, Luis Alejandro Velasco, manages to get to a life raft. He survives ten days at sea, fighting off sharks, without drinking water. He claims to, during a hallucination, eat the leather of his shoes. After he is rescued, he is welcomed as a hero, until the tide of public opinion turns and he is condemned as a liar. People say his story is so far-fetched that it can't possibly be true—he never could have survived the way and for as long as he claims. The last line of *The Story of a Shipwrecked Sailor*, the book García Márquez writes in Velasco's voice, reads: "Some people tell me this story is a fantasy. And I ask them: If it is, then what did I do during my ten days at sea?"

SUMMER 1985: Your girlfriend Sasha is the most sexual woman you have been with. Not that you've been with many people in your nineteen years. You are loaded every day and begin to have trouble keeping up with her, so you start on what passes for a health kick for a drug addict. You're taking massive amounts of vitamins—sometimes getting injections from a guy known, depending on who's referring to him, as "the band doctor" or "the junkie doctor." At this point, you are naïve enough to think he's an actual doctor. You say this to a friend, who laughs at you and calls you a simp.

Sasha grew up in the south of France and looks like Jeanne Moreau fresh off the screen from *Elevator to the Gallows*. You hear Miles Davis's astounding soundtrack from that film pulsing and rushing through you every time you look into her eyes. You are still young and somewhat nervous about sex—that the person who wants you might stop wanting you ten seconds later if you do the wrong thing. She laughs about this and calls you "my little American," and if it were chemically possible, you would, in fact, *melt* when she says this. "Such a shy boy, my little American."

You are shy. The only time you talk to strangers is when you are loaded. Though, you are always loaded.

The night you meet at a party, Sasha tells you she does not believe in monogamy. She does not believe in labels, like *heterosexual, homosexual, bisexual*.

She says, "I like to be honest here. No surprises." And you feel a rare swelling of pride, so you tell her you're an addict and a drunk. *I am as liberated and honest as Sasha*, you think.

She makes a face, ignoring your confession. "*Hetero*-sexual. *Homo*sexual. *Bi*sexual." She shakes her head. "I am Sexual."

No debate there.

You and Sasha fuck in the small bedroom in the apartment you share with your friend Concetta. You like Concetta, you care deeply for her, maybe love her—but this is during a long period of your life when you mistake needing people for loving people. You mistake your constant desperate need for being romantic. At any rate, your attraction has no reciprocation, as Concetta most certainly DOES believe in labels—labels such as *lesbian*.

You and Concetta talk at breakfast sometimes after Sasha has gone to work.

"That is one amazing fucking woman," Concetta says.

You nod.

Concetta kids you about how great Sasha's blow jobs must be.

"How would you know?" you say.

"You think I'm deaf? I *hear* you. When you fuck, I hear *her*. What a fucking voice that girl has." Concetta stops. Sips her coffee. "I think about fucking your girlfriend. I hope that's okay." She lights a cigarette. "Anyway, when I don't hear her, all I hear are the loudest and the fucking goofiest and most pathetically grateful orgasms I have *ever* heard."

"Since when are you an expert on the sounds of guys' orgasms?"

"I have *heard* plenty of men come," she says. "I have even—I hope to fucking god for the last time—*made* men come. Not that it's the most difficult thing on the planet."

After a week of taking huge "treatments" of B12 and various other vitamin shots in the ass, you are sleeping more often from the sedatives the quack doctor gives you. You are actually looking and feeling better than you have in a long time.

This is a little remarkable, really, since you are still drunk and loaded every day. Prior to the "treatments" your liver seemed to be backing up with toxins. Your skin was the color of an elephant's hide; your eyes were bloodshot and you couldn't breathe through your nose. You'd messed up the membranes too much to snort your drugs and you had to use other methods you really don't prefer. Now, for you, anyway, you feel incredible. The only downside is that this health kick *does* put a dent in your drug money. Still, you think the vitamins are a pretty great discovery.

Until later when Sasha is going down on you. After you come—in what, you now can't help thinking of as a *loud, goofy, and pathetically grateful orgasm*—Sasha sits up and makes a disgusted face like she's just eaten a handful of rancid pistachios. Not her usual reaction. She looks left, then right and you can tell something is terribly wrong. She gags and coughs onto the floor—also the opposite of her usual reaction. She wipes the back of her hand on her lips and sniffs her wrist and forearm, wincing again.

"You are taking vitamins?" she says.

"Not anymore, I'm not."

Later, you tell Concetta what happened. Between peals of laughter, she gives you some of the best advice you will ever get. "Listen. You are not healthy *anyway*, no matter how well you think that shit made you feel. The odds of you finding something other than vitamins that are good for you are pretty good. The odds of finding a woman who makes you sound the way you sound when you come with her are not very good at all."

She opens two beers and gives you one. "I'd say lose the fucking vitamins. Or give me her number."

You never take a vitamin again.

APRIL 15, 1912: Among the more than one thousand people who die in the sinking of the *Titanic* is Thomas Andrews, the marine architect who designed the ship, who becomes one of the few people in history killed by something they conceived and created.

1983: You have scars you lie about and scars you tell the truth about.

The summer you're seventeen, you tell people, you get chased by several cops for more than half an hour through the woods of your hometown. The same woods—though you don't think about this until later—that Nicole was killed in when you were eleven. You don't even remember why they were chasing you. You do remember being drunk. You remember the woods being dark and your body flooded with adrenaline and fear and sprinting over wet mossy stones and through the giant knuckled limbs of the trees. You hear them running behind you and you see the blur of their flashlights jumping up and down as they chase you.

You turn to look back and see if they're getting closer and you get clotheslined by a thick broken tree limb. Your head and chest stop. Your legs fly out in front of you and you're instantly on your back and your head hits the ground hard. You have trouble breathing, but know you have to get moving. You run for another five or ten minutes and end up hiding in tall grass on the dammed-up side of the lake. You stay there with just your head above the water. You listen for a while until, finally, the cops give up and you hear their footsteps grow more and more distant. Soon you can only hear the crickets in the woods and the fish gently surfacing and feeding on bugs and you hear and feel your heart beating and your breathing, hard at first and then more calmly.

You walk about a mile to a friend's house and see in her bathroom mirror that you've opened a slice across your collarbone so deep you can see the milky gray-white of your bone, so wide you can fit your index finger into the cut and feel your bone through the split skin and severed muscle. Touching the bone makes you queasier than looking at it does. Your shirt is soaked with blood and lake water. Your friend gives you a washcloth and you press it to the cut.

When you take it away and look in the mirror, you see the clean cut and the gray-white bone and then the blood pools again and all you see is red. And you press the washcloth against it for a while.

This story is true.

1987: You have a round scar about the size of a quarter between the thumb and forefinger of your left hand—white around the circumference and a deep red in the middle. People ask about it and you tell them some guy was pissed at you and had a friend hold you down while he burned you with a cigar. You will tell this same story for years. People seem to believe it. You're a fuckup. You've pissed off some angry people in the past.

This is a lie.

You give yourself the scar, burning your hand in the same spot repeatedly with the car cigarette lighter. You sit in your car and see your breath collect in puffs in the cold. You've got the key turned so that the electric is on but the engine is off. The car is dark. The streetlights glow a faded overexposed sepia on the rounded hills of snow that people have shoveled from their driveways and sidewalks. The Green Line train clatters on its tracks a couple of blocks away. You push the seat back and recline so much that you're almost lying down. You've learned already that you have to be comfortable if pain is going to feel good.

You pull the cigarette lighter out and it glows orange. You put your left hand on your thigh because you worry you'll jerk away from the lighter if you don't brace it against something, but your hand never moves as you press the lighter into that web of skin. It makes the same sound as Hawaiian lava when it joins the surf. The first time, you are surprised that it smells sweet and pleasant. You thought burning skin smelled horrible, but you were wrong—it's body hair that makes burns smell so bad. You are reminded of this years later when you get your first brand and Gayle holds your hand and kisses you and you are not at all alone and you smell your burning skin again and you think of being in that car by yourself.

The pain flashes and at first a chill shoots through your whole body, and then it's as if the lighter is a drug being injected at the burn and you feel an incredibly calm, beautiful peace radiate from your hand into every cell of your body. Pain hurts when you don't expect it, when you resist it. When you know it's coming and you relax into it, you and the pain move together and it's like you and the lighter make a complete electrical circuit that allows a current to flow through. Let it happen, you learn, and it feels good everywhere. Every jumpy, fractured nerve is smoothed by the pain. And all the hurt evaporates for a little while.

When the lighter loses its heat, you take it away from your skin and reset it. The windows are fogged up and the streetlights are an expressionist blur now. When the lighter clicks to let you know it's ready to go again, you light a cigarette and crack the window and feel the cold air, and you smoke and let your head fall, heavy and spent, against the headrest. There is no tension left in your body. You breathe the smoke in deeply.

It's years before you tell anyone how you really get that scar. Now it seems ridiculous that you wouldn't have told someone what you did to yourself, but you are not the same person you used to be. Except, of course, when you are.

2010: You're on your way home from an AA meeting in Palm Springs (your home group, which you attend every week) and you hit a traffic jam. Two lanes are down to one and there are cop lights ahead. You think you can go into the left lane and cut across through the grocery-store parking lot, but after you have swerved out of your lane and passed several cars, you realize it's not possible. You try to get back into the single-lane flow of traffic. A cop comes over and beats on your door.

"What? You think you're some asshole who the rules don't apply to?" he screams at you.

You try to explain yourself. That you weren't trying to cut ahead of the other cars but trying to get into the parking lot.

"How much have you been drinking tonight?"

You laugh.

"What the fuck is so funny?" His anger reminds you of every small-time jerk with authority who has ever yelled at you.

"I've been at an AA meeting," you say.

"AA meeting? That's a great one. Yeah. I've never heard that."

You look up at him. His gray-white skin flashes shades of blue and red from the cruiser lights.

He says, "Get out of the car."

"What?"

"Get out of your fucking car!"

Before you know what's happening, he has you face-down on your hood and he's going through your wallet. He tells you not to move while he calls you in. You're shaking. There's really nothing to be afraid of. There's no information he can "call in" on you. Nobody wants you for anything. No matter how long the odds may have once been, you're a respectable citizen. Still, you're afraid. You know that cops don't need any real cause to bring you in for anything, and this guy seems to have it in for you. You find yourself thinking, *Fucking low-rent loser. Get a fucking life. Go arrest someone who's done something, for Christ's sake.* But you are in a familiar position of powerlessness with a man who seems irate at you for reasons you can't fathom. You feel the heat from your engine warming your cheek on the hood. Your legs are spread uncomfortably, but you are afraid to move.

He comes back and pulls you roughly upright. He gives you back your wallet.

"Stop driving like a fucking asshole," he says.

You stand there. Not knowing what you are allowed to say to this man.

"Get the fuck out of here," he says.

You get in your car, your legs still shaking.

1972: Your grandfather on your father's side is from Halifax. On April 16, 1912, the day after the *Titanic* sinks, the

White Star Line sends the *Mackay-Bennett*—known as "the undertaker ship"—from Halifax to the last known coordinates of the *Titanic*. It's tasked with claiming the bodies floating in the twenty-eight-degree water, loading them onto the ship stocked with as many pine caskets as it can carry—though still not enough for the bodies there—and, ultimately, bringing them back to Halifax for burial. A family friend of your grandfather's is eighteen years old and on his first White Star Line job. He tells your grandfather about the debris fields—two large ones, which have given some credence to the much-debated eyewitness accounts that the ship did in fact split in two prior to sinking—littered with tables and deck chairs and wooden luggage crates and the swollen bodies of the dead. His job is to judge what class the victims sailed based on the quality of their clothing. First-class victims are given priority and immediately taken aboard. Second-class victims are taken on a case-by-case basis as a result of the *Mackay-Bennett*'s dwindling number of caskets. Steerage passengers are loaded down with weights and sunk.

Your grandfather's family friend was prepared for the bodies. It was the job he signed up for, after all. The bodies of the passengers aren't what disturbed him. What he never forgets, though, is the dull clunk against the side of the ship, fishing a stiff corpse from the water. It is not human. It's a frozen Labrador retriever. Many first-class passengers were traveling with pets. He brings it halfway up the ship's side, sees what he has taken from the water, and places it gently, gently for reasons he's never sure of, back in the freezing water. He watches it until it is a dot on the horizon as the ship moves to the perimeter of the debris field, looking for more bodies. The image of the frozen dog is the one that stays with him.

1977: Three Girl Scouts are murdered June 12 in Oklahoma. You learn about their deaths when you are researching Nicole's case. These murders happen ten days before Nicole is killed. The cases are unrelated, of course, but share the fact that they are both unsolved. The Girl Scouts are between the ages of eight and ten. They are raped and murdered and left near their camp tent. Gene Leroy Hart, a violent ex-con and escapee, is tried for the crime and acquitted. Thirty years later DNA samples are tested but are too degraded and the results prove inconclusive.

1986: You are working at the Marlboro Market and your boss sends you out for the weekend's change. There aren't many bank machines. Besides, you need enough quarters and dimes and nickels and pennies to make change for Saturday and Sunday. He sends you to the bank. On the way back, you are walking down Massachusetts Avenue with more than a thousand dollars in bills and coins and an enormous man is walking toward you. You realize too late that he isn't just some guy who doesn't see you—he's coming at you with purpose. He looks like Chief from *One Flew over the Cuckoo's Nest* and he must have a hundred pounds on you and he towers over you by nearly a foot. Before you realize what's happening, he punches you in the chest. The sack of money goes flying, but doesn't break or open. At first, you think he must have seen you come from the bank and that he's robbing you. But then he just stands over you, staring down into your eyes. He doesn't take the money.

"What are you going to do about it?" he says.

He's waiting for an answer. You think of all the men who have scared the shit out of you in your life. You say, "Nothing."

1990: You are living in Sarasota, Florida. In the last year, you have lived in Amherst, Massachusetts (where you were in and dropped out of an MFA program), Marathon in the Florida Keys, and now Sarasota. Months from now you will be living in your car, parking as often as you can in beach parking lots on the Gulf of Mexico, and then in a freezing house filled with tweakers you don't know in Winston-Salem, North Carolina. For now, though, you haven't totally worn out your welcome in Sarasota. Your relationship with Mary is ending, but you are still together. You and Mary have been together, on and off, for years. You've moved to Florida to be with her, where she's studying at some design school. You have no reason to be in Florida at all except to be with Mary, and this is taxing your relationship, along with the fact that you are falling deeper into your addictions. You're barely having sex anymore, though you fall asleep, drunk, holding each other often, still. She's recently shaved her head and you find yourself gently kissing the mitten-shaped scar on her head while she sleeps.

Your life hasn't totally fallen apart yet. You are starting to realize it's going to, though. You are beginning to feel helpless. For years, you have romanticized being a fuckup, but now you're starting to see there's a real cost. You could lose Mary. And not much else matters to you at this point. But you can't stop yourself.

1991: Your friend Sharon throws a party. She's a veterinary assistant and she's swiped a bunch of liquid ketamine and you are filled with ketamine and beer and you couldn't get off the couch if you wanted to. Sharon asks you to pass her the TV remote. You realize you can't move. You wonder if your involuntary muscles will stop working, too. You think you might die. You could stop breathing. You could stop swallowing.

"Dude, what's your fucking problem?" Sharon says. "Give me the clicky."

You think you are dying. Even if you aren't dying on your own, you know that Sharon owns a python named Axel that she lets roam free in the house. You hate snakes. You fear snakes that kill people by constricting their ability to breathe far more than you fear poisonous snakes, though to be fair you are afraid of all snakes. But pythons are the worst. You fear losing your breath, you fear drowning. You fear emphysema, though that doesn't stop you from smoking, since you don't plan on living to thirty anyway.

Sharon say, "You are deep in a K-hole, dude."

All you can move are your eyes. You are alive. You are breathing if you can still hear Sharon. You wonder where Axel is. You can't talk. That snake could be anywhere. It could wrap itself around you and you'd be dead.

You may not plan on seeing thirty, but you're only

twenty-five. You are going to pick the way you go. You'll OD or drive your car off a cliff into the ocean. That, you have already decided.

1903: Ed Delahanty, a professional baseball player, is drunk when he drowns in Niagara Falls. There is some debate over whether he jumped or was pushed. He was often referred to as unstable and thought to have suffered from some form of mental illness.

1986: You play once—maybe twice—with one of the guys from the Boston band Dumptruck. They have recently broken up. You loved them. One of your favorite records is *D Is for Dumptruck*. They were too good to be just a local band. They should have made it.

Here's how it happens: After Dumptruck splits, a friend introduces you to one of the guitar players. She says to you both at a bar you're all drinking at that you guys will really click, musically and personally.

You end up scheduling a time to play with him and a couple of other guys. When you play together you are nervous—this guy was in Dumptruck! But you play well. He has some really complimentary things to say, says he loved how it sounded and that you should play together more. But you don't.

Over the years, you will say that you almost played in Dumptruck. Sometimes the lie will grow and you will say that you played in the band the guy did after Dumptruck. Once, you will tell someone that you were *in* Dumptruck, but there's no recorded evidence because they were involved in some legal issues with the record company after they released *D Is for Dumptruck* and they could only play live gigs. This last lie is—legally, at any rate—totally believable. Another time, you tell the same lie about being in Dumptruck when they were being sued, and add that you, as a member of the band, are part of the suit, even though you weren't *in* the band when the legal trouble started.

You played maybe a couple of times with a guy who was in a pretty obscure Boston band in the mid-1980s. It's 1991, in Sarasota, Florida. No one knows who the hell Dumptruck was or is. The guy you are lying to—a waiter in the restaurant where you cook—would probably believe you if you told him you were the whole genius *behind* Dumptruck. But you keep your lies pretty small.

You were in the guitar player from Dumptruck's later band. Or, you were briefly *in* Dumptruck, but there are no recordings, which is a real tragedy, because you were a great live band.

You never lie about being in the band during their heyday. You never say you were in any bands *bigger* than Dumptruck, which was not very big even at its peak. Even your lies, elaborate as they may get, are not full of ambition.

2011: You decide that, with or without the help of the Monroe cops, you must find out more about Nicole's murder. You've been waking up, shaking, seeing images of her dead body. Images, of course, that you never saw in real life. Your birthday's coming up, which is also the anniversary of her murder, and it always gets you down. You wake up on your birthday and remember Nicole's murder and it clouds the day.

What you think you remember:

You think Nicole had a younger brother and her mother became enormously protective of him after Nicole's murder. You think you remember that the mother made him take self-defense classes from a very young age. This may or may not be true. It makes sense. You think you remember hearing it. It sounds true, whether or not it happened.

You think your first boss—he ran the local florist and fruit market and hired you when you were fourteen to dig potatoes while paying you something like fifty cents an hour—found her body. This may be true. It may not be.

You are almost positive that Nicole's mother moved away not long after the murder. But you may only think this is logical, which, of course, doesn't make it true. You don't remember ever seeing her after the murder. But you don't remember seeing her before the murder, either. You'd only ever seen Nicole at school and after school with the other kids.

Here's what you find out from the articles:

There are rumors that the police had a strong suspect and that there was a torn piece of a T-shirt not far from the crime scene. Why no one has ever done a DNA test is beyond you. And of course they would have, if there were evidence to test. Some DA would love to close a thirty-four-year-old murder of a little girl. This calls into question whether or not there even is a T-shirt. From what you find in your research, however, there is no reason to doubt that there was a strong suspect, but not enough evidence to ever make a case. You consider who this suspect might be.

You think of one enormously creepy guy who was in his twenties and always hitting on ten- to twelve-year-old girls. He had some kind of head injury and everyone seemed to feel bad for him. As you remember it, he exposed himself to a ten-year-old girl at your town park and his father, who was connected with the local mob guys, got him off.

You ask your father where this guy lived, wondering if his house was close to Nicole's. Your dad has no idea. You find him on Facebook. He has nothing but pictures of himself—usually shirtless, bodybuilding shots—and famous Disney stars when they were younger, like Miley Cyrus around age twelve. Britney Spears on *The All New Mickey Mouse Club*. Christina Aguilera.

You think, *It's not out of the question*. You think you could maybe crack the case, solve a thirty-four-year-old murder. Of course, this is absurd. How could you?

You find every newspaper article you can. The earliest are dated June 23, 1977, the day after she went missing between 6:00 and 6:20 p.m. Her body was found only hours later. Some articles are from years afterward. You find one that has an interview with the officer in charge of the case, long after it happened. Monroe is not a big town. They don't have a cold case unit, only this one officer who stays familiar with the case for decades. In an interview with a local paper on the twentieth anniversary of her murder, he says that Nicole's mother would call every year on her birthday and ask if there had been any leads or progress on

her case. Every year he had to tell her the same thing—
they knew no more than they did in 1977. She calls on
Nicole's birthday for seven years, always getting the same
answer.

Then she stops calling.

You wonder why you are so obsessed with this. It's *Nicole's mother's* story. Not yours. You're pretty sure you never
met the woman. Maybe if she found out some stranger was
digging into the case it would hurt her. But for some reason, you are haunted by Nicole in your early forties. You
dream about her head being bludgeoned. You obsess over
the case. You read about it as much as you can. Your fear of
men returns, though it's not as strong as it was in the years
following her murder. Nicole is a story in your life.

But she is not only your story, and she is not nearly as
much yours as she is her mother's. Her brother's. If they're
still alive, are you capable of hurting them?

2011: You find yourself, when looking around the room at
one of your regular AA meetings while you still live in the
desert you hate, on the verge of an anxiety attack. You think
you may need to take a Xanax before the attack peaks. You
are having trouble breathing, and you are thinking about
how much you fear some of the men at the meeting. It's not
a thought you like. These people are supposed to be your
peers, after all. You're there to help one another. Not judge
one another. But you've been finding yourself full of fear
in rooms with men who talk—and sometimes even seem
like they're bragging—about their violent pasts. And there
are a ton of violent men at your meeting. You find yourself

going to meetings where there are more women. Daytime meetings tend to have fewer men. You start going to them. Increasingly, even though you know it's not wise, you just skip the meetings altogether.

1985–1993: Over the course of about a decade, you have two serious long-term relationships. Both of these women are very understanding about the fact that you're often medicated. They know you're bipolar. They are very forgiving—even if you yourself are not—of how these pills fuck with your libido and your dick. Men in their fifties, you think, have to deal with their cocks not working. Why you? Why in your twenties? You hate your fucking brain.

When you are single, you go off your meds. It's one thing to suffer through a limp dick with a woman who loves you—it's another to do it with a stranger. That would be violating part of the contract of casual sex.

You later find out that these weekends of sleeping with three different women are not, in fact, just you having a good time. You learn that you are dead center in manic episodes when you fuck around. You read that for a manic episode to be diagnosed, several factors occur at once:

- Expanded self-esteem.
- "Pressured speech"—characterized by rapid bursts, often jumping from topic to topic.
- Severely reduced need for sleep—two or three hours a night is common. Days without any need to sleep can occur, though you pay a horrible price when the episode is over.

- Overindulgence and risky behavior in enjoyable things like sex, drugs, alcohol, and shopping.

You have no idea that promiscuity is a symptom of anything. You just think you get laid a lot and you really don't see a problem. Because you're getting laid a lot.

You stay up, sleeping an hour or two a night, for a week or two at a time with your energy flying, your self-esteem off the charts.

Then you crash terribly. You can't get out of bed. It's like gravity has quadrupled its force. You can't bother to shave or shower. You barely leave the house, drinking alone at home. Eventually it starts all over, and suddenly you want to be back out and around people. You're up for days. You're always looking for something or someone new. You are addicted to alcohol and opiates and sex and new adventures.

You have friends dropping from AIDS, but you still never use a condom. One night a friend, a woman you have slept with on two occasions, comes to see you at work, holding a *Time* magazine with a picture of the HIV virus on the cover. She's in medical school. She knows shit.

She says, "We're all going to die."

You don't really know what to say to this.

"There's no stopping this virus," she says. "It adapts to each host."

"Don't all viruses do that?"

"They don't all kill you," she says.

You've already lost three friends. You expect you'll lose a lot more—quickly. You are twenty. You think about dying more than most people you know. But somehow you don't think this is what's going to get you in the end.

You look at the photo of the virus. It is, like so many things out of context, beautiful.

It's like the MRIs you will later see of your brain. The bipolar brain lights up and fires differently than a normal brain. At your particular baseline—which is a state known as hypomania—your brain looks like a lovely planet covered with an electrical storm. A green-and-red planet with glowing white-hot veins firing, connecting everything. It looks incredible, impossibly beautiful. It's where all your trouble lies.

1991: You work in the kitchen at a catering company. You have to be there at ten every morning. Often, you puke blood when you wake up. Every day, you need two or three drinks to stop your shaking hands, so you can be ready for work. You are drinking on your breaks, just to keep from getting sick during the day. You are exhausted all the time. You need to quit, you tell yourself. But you can't seem to do it, and you keep on the way you've been going.

2013: You tell the story about your grandfather and the family friend who worked on the *Mackay-Bennett*, the ship that goes to fish out the bodies in the twenty-eight-degree water.

Some facts:

- Your grandfather is from Halifax.
- The day after the *Titanic* sinks, the White Star Line

sends what is known as "the undertaker ship," the *Mackay-Bennett*, from Halifax to the last known coordinates of the *Titanic*, where it will claim the bodies left floating in the twenty-eight-degree water, load them onto the ship, and bring them to Halifax for burial.

- The ship does not have enough pine caskets to hold the bodies left on the surface.
- There are two debris fields littered with tables and deck chairs and wooden luggage crates and, of course, the bodies of the dead. These two distinct fields give some credence to eyewitness claims that the ship split in two prior to sinking.
- Crew members of the ship are to judge by the quality of the victims' clothing what class they were. First-class victims are given priority and taken immediately to caskets. Second-class victims are taken on a case-by-case basis due to the dwindling number of coffins. Steerage passengers are loaded down with weights and sunk. This decision is based on the logic that there would be no one in Halifax to claim the poorer bodies because they were coming to America to start a new life. This is a much-debated fact—whether or not the bodies were fished out of the water by class.

The lies:

- The family friend who tells the story.
- The frozen dog.

You make up the family friend to justify why you would tell the story beyond your own weird obsession. The frozen dog makes it human. Less factual, yes, but for you more true and memorable. Without the frozen dog, it's not a story. It's just history.

5

2004: You are on your hands and knees, your wrists are bound, and you are being caned. The first ten or twenty strikes sting badly—they are just pain. A pain you have to get through for the pain to get you where you need to be. You are blindfolded and you hear the authoritative click of your wife's heels on the wood floor as she walks around you. With each strike, your whole body lurches forward and your ass stings and you wince. Slowly, around twenty strikes in, your body begins to relax and you ride with the pain and stop fighting it. Soon, you are not moving at all when the cane hits your ass and you are emitting a low moan that you can't control. She starts hitting you harder. Each blow radiates a calm throughout your body. You feel your skin grow tight and you know that there are welts rising on your ass.

"Just breathe," your wife says.

You take deep breaths. The tension melts from your body.

She hits you again and you don't move at all.

Your eyes are closed, even though you're blindfolded, and you are breathing calmly and every time you are hit you let out a low, animalistic groan of pleasure that spills from your mouth. Your body feels like it's floating. It's as good as heroin. With each strike, you feel everything that worries you or scares you or haunts you leaving your body and all that's left is you, peaceful, no matter how hard you're being hit.

2005: You and Gayle are having dinner with another couple, very good friends of yours. You think you are close. Dinner talk turns to sex. In the course of conversation, you and your wife mention you're into S/M and that you are the one into pain. Either you or your wife mentions that you have a brand with Gayle's initials. This doesn't seem to cause any trouble at dinner, but the next day you get an e-mail from one of your friends saying she is worried about you—that she thinks you're in an abusive relationship. At first you think this is a joke, that she's kidding, but it soon becomes clear that she is serious. She tells you that she and her husband are concerned. You think she's being ridiculous and put it out of your mind. Until you realize that they no longer accept your invitations to dinner, nor do they invite you and Gayle to dinner.

You had seen each other regularly, spoken often. You realize the friend still e-mails you but not your wife. She has taken some judgmental stance on Gayle, freezing her out, and this angers and hurts you.

At one point, the two of you are out for coffee and you tell her that you have a terrible headache.

She says, "I thought you liked pain."

You look at her. "You are joking, right?"

She isn't joking. She thinks you just like any pain that happens to cross your path. It hits you that she's really clueless about all this and it begins to anger you even more that she's making judgments based on such a level of ignorance.

"I don't get turned on when I have a headache," you say. "*Nobody* on the planet gets a hard-on when they have a headache." You shake your head.

She says, "It doesn't seem healthy. What you're doing."

You can't believe you're having this conversation. These are liberals. They would never dream of judging a gay friend who had come out to them, hiding under the guise of concern.

Your friendship with this woman is over. You have no patience for people who judge you. You have even less patience for people who judge your wife.

Before the check has come for the coffee, you have decided you have spoken with her for the last time. This isn't a friend.

Years later, you will make up with this woman, realizing you misread the dinner conversation. You were thinking they would want to hear something they didn't want to hear. You will feel guilty for having brought the whole thing up. You didn't realize it at the time, but you will come to realize that you had as much to do with hurting this friend-

ship as they did. You wonder how much of this—the bipolar, the addiction, the S/M—people in your life simply
do not want to hear. How many relationships you may be
blowing apart with this, and it frightens you.

1993: You move to Buffalo to be near Gayle after you have
been long-distance lovers for more than six months. You
take an apartment down the street from hers, but you end
up spending every night in her apartment. You only spend
time in your place twice—once to write an unpublishable
story and once to watch the Knicks lose in triple overtime
to the Magic. You later call it the most expensive writing
office you have ever had.

After a month, you still haven't found a job and you realize there's no way you can afford to keep your apartment.
You think you will have to move back into your grandmother's hoarder house, still filled with her shit no matter
how many trips to the dump you've taken. Another winter
there alone feels unimaginable. You've only been sober for
five months. You have no idea if you can stay sober alone.
And you don't want to leave Gayle. You're afraid of going
back to being long-distance. Afraid you'll lose her.

You tell her that you'll have to leave Buffalo. That you
can't afford it and you'll have to go back to the farmhouse
in Connecticut filled with your grandmother's lifetime of
garbage and ugly memories.

You have fantasies that you could just stay here and live
with Gayle, in her orderly apartment, and the two of you
could build some kind of life together, a kind you've never
quite had, although you've lived with women before. You

think about all the people you've lived with, many of whom you didn't even particularly like. Moving in with Gayle would be a no-brainer for you. You like her tremendously. You think you might be falling in love. But you know what Gayle's independence means to her. She has never had a roommate, male or female, never come anywhere close to moving in with a lover. You are not sure whether she *ever* wants to move in with a man, or whether a life as a self-sufficient woman on her own is the one she pictures for herself, so different from her mother, who has been financially dependent on her father her entire adult life, and who at times suffers from agoraphobia, making her dependent on her husband and kids in other ways too.

Gayle loves her mother and is close to her, but you know she has spent most of her life since her teens focused on becoming a different kind of woman, standing on her own two feet and proving herself. So moving in with a guy she's just started dating, a guy who doesn't even have a job, does not strike you as something this sort of woman would even consider.

That night you make love. You hold each other all night. Both of you are crying.

Sometime around dawn, Gayle sits up and says, "You could stay here."

It doesn't seem possible that she is really saying this. It is one of those rare moments in life when it feels like the world has somehow read your mind and you have made something—with the sheer force of your desire—manifest into reality.

"Really?" you say, afraid that she cannot mean it—that she must be just being polite, and you are supposed to decline. But you don't want to decline.

She smiles around her tears. "Really," she says. Her eyes make her look as happy as you are.

And you move in together. Friends of yours tell you you're being impulsive and that you're on the rebound from Mary and you're less than six months sober and that it's dangerous to move in with someone you've only been seeing long-distance for a few months. But you and Gayle have been friends for years. You've never been with someone you feel quite this way about. And you have nowhere else left to go. You move in together.

2000: You are spending your first night in the first house that you and your wife have just bought. It's a beaten-down 1912 California bungalow in a somewhat seedy section of Long Beach that you bought for $115,000—a price tag that both stuns your friends and makes them afraid to visit you. "It must be in a fucking combat zone," one says.

The first night, you are awake, unable to stop your mind from spinning while Gayle sleeps beside you.

You get up. You walk through the rooms, still filled with packed boxes against the walls and hastily arranged furniture. You walk out onto the porch. There's a fog coming off the ocean, ten blocks south, and the air smells like salt and your skin beads with moisture as you sit on the porch under the orange glow of the streetlight on your corner.

You think: *Ten years ago I was sleeping in my car.*

You feel like Gatsby. You own a house. You are clean and sober. There are no collection agencies after you. You don't have to be afraid of a cop if you walk past one—although you still *are* afraid of cops. You have a career. You teach college classes. You are happily married.

Ten years ago if someone had told you that you would be sitting on this porch, you would never have believed them. You don't even recognize your own life.

You smell the air. The streetlight hums. You stay where you are. On, you remind yourself, *your* porch.

2013: Your parents will not talk about either your addictions or your mental illness, and haven't in more than twenty years. They seem ashamed that you're an addict. You don't really know your mother's reasons and you never will. Your father was a narcotics officer and must be embarrassed that his son fell in with drugs.

But their silence about your bipolar bothers you more.

When you have had five episodes this year, you decide to try again and talk to your parents about your brain. When your father asks you how you've been, you answer honestly and tell him you've been having some trouble with your bipolar. He doesn't say anything. When you try telling your mother, you are even more honest, telling her you've had a really tough year and that you've had "a couple" of manic episodes. You are careful to not say the word *psychotic*. She changes the subject.

Your parents are good people. They are generous. They have constantly helped you, in more ways than you can count. And where they haven't helped, they have done their best. You don't hold any anger toward them. You defend them to friends who are really blunt and harsh when they talk about how your parents ignore something so central to your existence.

You also make apologies to yourself for them. If they knew how bad it could be—if you told them everything— they would have to talk about it. They love you. They give a shit. But the way they handle it becomes a gulf between you.

You know you're done talking about it with them. It's not something they want to hear, and it's no longer something you will try to talk about.

1993: You and Gayle have been living together about six months when she complains about how messy you are. You don't think you're that messy, maybe a little cluttered, but you come from two generations of people who never throw shit away. There's your hoarder grandmother, of course. And your parents' house, Gayle will later see, is an embarrassing mess. When she does see their house, she will actually tell you that you are surprisingly neat, given what you've come from.

But this day, she says, "You have to be neater. I like my house the way I like it."

You remind yourself that Gayle has never had a roommate. She lived at home during college and has lived alone her whole time in grad school. You have had more than fifty roommates, not counting the tweakers in the commune in

Winston-Salem. You think about all the slobs you've lived with, the addicts and thieves and people whose lives were falling apart around them. You are amazed at her life. She has a bank account and pays bills on time. She's organized. Everything has a place. She doesn't leave her books all over, several at a time, their spines cracked on every flat surface.

"I've lived with a lot of people," you tell her. "Really. I'm not that bad a person to live with."

But you are afraid maybe you will be too tough to live with. And she will want you gone. You love her and she feels like your last chance. You tell her you'll try to be better.

2007: Your hands grow sore from massaging Gayle every night, but you have run out of other ideas. Nothing works. At this point, you are only weeks away from starting to steal her pain medication. Within the last year, she has tried acupuncture, Ayurveda healing, various exercises; she has joined support groups only to find that the people in support groups drove her crazy and to realize that she didn't want to live a life defined by her illness. She can no longer lift weights. She can no longer do any exercise that breaks down her muscles or she goes into a pain flare that puts her in total agony from head to toe. The only thing that helps is swimming in a heated pool.

There is no way you can afford a heated pool in Los Angeles County, so you end up moving to Desert Hot Springs, three hours from your friends. Three hours from your work and your life—from any readings or shows or events in LA. It's a town of twenty-five thousand people. You have never lived anywhere with fewer than half a million people since leaving home at eighteen, except when you were alone in your grandmother's hoarder house. You love cities. But this is for your wife. You love her. You think of all she's done for you over the years. You're no cakewalk, with your depression and brain. Marriage is a partnership. Plus, if this makes her well, it's a choice you would make a hundred times out of a hundred.

So you don't think twice about leaving Long Beach. Maybe you should, but you don't. You find a house the first day you look in Desert Hot Springs. You are leaving a 1912 Arts and Crafts bungalow that you two have restored, a home that you both love, for a cookie-cutter house that you can't stand the sight of.

But you don't really think much about this. You don't even consider that it could send you into an unfixable depression. Instead, you think that this might put Gayle in remission. This could be what cures her. Anything is worth that.

You move in October, months after you have already relapsed, though Gayle is unaware of this. You surprise yourself twice, if only because you don't tend to cry over things:

You cry when you take a last look at the interior of your Long Beach house.

And you wake up teary-eyed the next day in the new house, wondering what you have done to end up there.

———

EARLY 1990S: You will lie to your parents that you need money for your student loans or your rent, or for some collection agency that's after you—you forget. The money is really for your brain meds that you can't afford because you don't have insurance. You feel bad for lying to them, but you think there's no way to be sure they would have given you the money for the meds (looking back, they probably would have), and you definitely need them, as you have had a couple of psychotic breaks and you are afraid of your brain.

Already you are sick of being the science experiment you will be for the rest of your life. The drugs start with small dosages and build up to the dosage they think may work. Then the drugs make you fat or stupid or they kill your cock, or they simply don't work, and you have to scale back on the ones that don't work and start the process over with some new drug.

2006: Your band, the Urinals, is opening for Yo La Tengo at the Fillmore in San Francisco. You can't believe it. Fifteen years ago, your life was in a shambles. Even ten years ago, sober, you'd given up on playing music with other people. This moment feels miraculous.

You know yourself. You know that you spend far too much of your time regretting your past or worrying about your future. You tell yourself, all night long, to pay attention. To appreciate this.

You are standing under the same chandelier that Jimi Hendrix stood under. On the same stage that Janis Joplin sang on. Pay attention, you tell yourself.

When Yo La Tengo has your band join them for the encore, you look out at 1,400 people dancing. Remember this, you tell yourself. Stay in this moment as long as you can.

1972: Your father is a pharmacist at Fairfield Hills State Hospital and for some reason he has taken you to work. You're bored. You end up crawling around on the floor and take a red pill that looks like candy. Before too long, you feel better than you ever have. Your brain and body float. It's like gravity has been defeated. You curl up in a blissed-out ball in the back corner of the pharmacy.

Another pharmacist—one who insists you call him Uncle Phil—finds you on the floor. You can barely make out words and images, but you are as happy as you have ever been. Everyone around you seems so concerned and you wonder why they couldn't have just left you where you were, feeling so good.

6

2013: You don't remember how you get a lot of your scars. You wake up for years from drunken and drugged blackouts with deep bruises and gashes and cuts. Friends tell you how you got some of them. Others still remain a mystery. You have told a lie about almost every one of them—whether you remember how you got them or not—to friends, to people at parties and in bars, to lovers who see you naked. Sometimes you tell the truth. Someone will ask about one of your scars and you will say you have no idea where it came from, and you feel better for having told the truth, but worse and deeply regretful that it *is* the truth. That you have wasted so many years of your life. That for years you only knew what you had done the night before because a friend or lover would tell you.

You find scars—yours or anyone else's—beautiful. One of your biggest and, you think, prettiest scars cuts across three inches on your left calf. This one you get accidentally while using a metal saw on a construction/destruction site when you work labor-pool jobs in Florida. It is seven in the morning. The day's yet to get brutally hot, though it's still so humid it feels like you're breathing through a damp blanket. You're drunk and you slice the jigsaw with the metal cutting blade across your calf.

There's a newer scar—a deep white line, red at its edges. You know how you got it, but have only told your best friend, Gina.

It's from swinging a heavy twelve-inch kitchen knife aimed at your left knuckle. You miss slightly, and the scar sits about a centimeter closer to the wrist than you'd expected. You do this in 2013. You easily could have severed a tendon that would seriously fuck up your ability to play guitar—one of the most important things in your life. You are totally sober. It's four and a half years since your relapse. You haven't been sleeping much for weeks, but you are not in an episode. You are not hearing voices. You are not seeing things. You have no idea why you do this.

You are still, for some reason, a danger to yourself at times. You are still capable of frightening yourself. After the knife hits, you are calm and it feels good as you bleed steadily onto the wood floor.

You think about Vic Chesnutt and his muscle relaxants and his conversation with Terry Gross. You think of all the times you have tried to kill yourself and that you were probably, in the end, chicken. But so was he and he finally did it. Who says you won't get there too? You're afraid of your own brain—but mostly you're afraid of the absence of that fear, because when it's gone and you're feeling in control, that's when you're in trouble.

For years you will wonder why you didn't kill yourself in your lowest, most desperate moments, and the best answer you come up with is: *I don't know.* This scares you and makes you wonder if you'll have a better answer if a next time comes around. Maybe you just got lucky. Maybe it's just that all living things have a drive to live. To adapt. From bacteria to viruses. Maybe you're no different. But it must be something more. You don't want to kill yourself now. Now you could make a list of things to live for. But what about the next time it gets unrelenting and you don't have that list, or the list is empty or meaningless? Then what? You need a better answer—that much you know. This part of the story is never over. You never know when or if you'll go back to that place again.

SPRING 1990: Even though you hate the bipolar meds, what you do to self-medicate is working less and less. Maybe not at all. Sometimes you can still stay up three or four days and nights writing or fucking or playing guitar, but less often than before. Various meds don't work. Some make you crazier. Some, when they do work, have terrible side effects.

Most times, you want to kill yourself—you think seriously, sometimes every night on the way home, about driving off the bridge from Turtle Bay in Sarasota, Florida, where you work. You frequently call in sick to work. You stay in bed for a week. You end up quitting a lot of jobs because you

can't work steady hours, and have to start getting up at—
or staying up until—five in the morning to work the labor
pool. You try to find a new job, but it's becoming harder and
harder to explain why a bright, educated person like you has
no references or job history from the last two years.

Generally, men and women about five years older than
you interview you for a job. They say things like, "And why
do you want to work at TGI Fridays?"

And you think about saying that your last job wasn't humiliating enough and that you aren't thinking nearly often
enough about killing yourself and you think working at
TGI Fridays might push you over the edge. Instead you say
nothing. Or you lie.

Most afternoons you wake up to friends' phone calls
telling you what you did the night before. Sometimes it's
funny. Sometimes it's horrifying and embarrassing. Sometimes it's frightening and you wonder how you survive
these nights. One afternoon, the night after your band plays
a show at some enormous loft that used to be a sewing-
machine factory, you wake up unable to form most words.
The ones you can say are incredibly slow, and inside your
head it sounds like an air-raid siren is going off six inches
from your ear. Your elbows are bloody and swollen and
your clothes are covered in solid crusty puke. When you
smell yourself, you throw up on the floor.

"You're cleaning that up," your roommate Mel says.

You gently touch the back of your head and your hair
is bunched and hard with blood and you wince when you
touch the bare, bloodied skin. You close your eyes and see
stars.

———

2010: An autopsy conducted on the brain of Owen Thomas, a twenty-one-year-old junior lineman at the University of Pennsylvania who committed suicide, showed early stages of CTE, making him the second-youngest person to be diagnosed with the condition.

1986: You have just come back from Holland and you want, desperately, to return. You have hated most of the years of your life and it is the only place you have ever felt at home. You tell your parents you are taking a semester off and going back to Amsterdam.

Your mother says they will not help you with tuition if you go now and try to come back in the fall. You have taken out a ton of student loans, but they have cosigned for some of them and they are paying a fair amount of your tuition. You like college. You cave in and go back to school.

But you totally fuck off. You rarely go to class. In Holland, you discovered opiates and now spend three or four months nodding off on your couch or your dealer's. One of the only things you will remember about this semester is being terribly dopesick when the *Challenger* explodes in the sky. One minute you are watching it explode, the next minute you are puking and shitting in your bathroom, where you spend hours.

You drink, you fuck, you get loaded and high all semester. Late in the term, you go to your professors and say you've been hospitalized, that your grandmother has died.

You tell one of them that your mother has died and you feel awful for even saying it, but it works.

Some of them let you slide. They give you withdraws. One gives you an F. Another gives you some lousy grade. They all seem to think you're lying but don't seem to care.

Because your parents are on the loan and are paying a lot of your tuition, your grades get sent to their address. For years you will tell people that you had a 0.85 semester that spring.

Your father says, "Well, you wanted to take a semester off and your mother wanted you to stay in school. It looks like you both got your wish."

Your friends will hear about your 0.85 semester. Many think you are making this up. That you are full of shit.

Then, in 2007, you are hired to teach at a university that requires your undergraduate transcripts. To your amazement, it turns out that in the spring of 1986, you had a 0.57 semester. Even worse than you remember.

2013: A friend tells you that in twenty-three of the last twenty-seven ring deaths in professional boxing, the father was the cornerman.

It makes sense. A fighter in trouble would never quit on his father—no matter what kind of relationship they had.

And a fighter unable to protect himself is too far gone. By the time a punch can kill you, you're not even conscious enough *to* quit. The fighter is helpless. Only the cornerman throwing in the towel can save him.

Twenty-three fathers didn't throw that towel.

SUMMER 1979: In what is probably your third concussion, you are knocked out in the first half of a basketball game at summer camp. You are playing one of your best games. You have more than twenty points in the first half—most in the first quarter, and when they start doubling you, you're getting assists by the bushel. On a steal and fast break, you go up against Malcolm. He has nicknamed you "Tom Pitty-Patty" because out of uniform, you mostly wear your Tom Petty and the Heartbreakers T-shirt from the *Damn the Tor-pedoes* tour. You're one of the only white kids at the camp and, not surprisingly, Tom Petty is not well known among the other campers, who tend to sport Earth, Wind & Fire and Ohio Players shirts and have posters of Isaac Hayes's glistening bald head on the walls and doors of their dorm rooms. You've known Malcolm for years—he's taken a liking to you since the fourth grade, the first time you met in a summer league camp. He protects you from other kids.

That doesn't mean, however, that he's going to let you score some easy layup over him. It's 1979. Coaches at this camp take the "no layup" rule seriously. If you don't throw a hard foul on a player when he's close to the hoop, you're going to end up yanked and screamed at by the coach.

You're not thinking of any of this. You're only thinking that you're in a sick zone, that it seems like the hoop's as big as a swimming pool and you can guess what everyone else on the court is going to do.

But you guess very wrong when you try to take the ball

into Malcolm's chest. He's a foot taller and solid. He probably has fifty pounds on you. The last thing you remember is trying to decide in that split second whether to pass the ball to the teammate on your left, pull up for a safe ten-foot bank shot, or take the ball straight to the hoop, figuring the worst you'll come away with is two free throws.

The last thing you hear is Malcolm saying, "Don't take that weak shit in here, Tom Pitty-Patty."

And then, nothing.

You wake up to your coach cupping your head in his hands, talking to you. You can't make out the words. Everything sounds the way it does when you first take a hit of nitrous oxide, which you have been doing for about a year at this point.

Then, for the first time, someone uses smelling salts on you. It's pretty amazing. You wake up fully. Your head hurts and you feel like you could sleep.

"You really got your bell rung," your coach says. "You ready to go?"

Of course you're ready to go. Guys who aren't ready to go get replaced by guys who are. It gets drilled into you from the start: You play hurt, you play sore, you sure as hell play when all that's happened is that you've taken a hit to the head.

He slaps your cheek twice. You see stars. He says, "That's what I want to hear."

You stand and your legs go rubbery. You barely stay up. You think you might puke.

You say, "How much time is left in the half?"

He laughs at you. "It's halftime. You've been out for twenty minutes."

He seems to think it's funny. To be fair, you don't think much of it, except that you're a beat slow and you throw up in a garbage pail off by the bleachers before the second half starts. You take the court and you and Malcolm give each other some five-step elaborate handshake you have only recently been allowed to learn.

He says, "You shoulda passed, Tom Pitty-Patty."

Talking is hard. "Yup."

"At least you hit the free throws."

"I shot free throws?" you say.

He laughs and hits you playfully in the chest with the back of his hand.

You try to remember shooting free throws, but no. It's gone. It must have happened, but you weren't there for it.

About five minutes into the half, you get run into a pick and your head snaps to the right and something crunches in your neck.

The next thing you remember is the second time someone uses smelling salts on you.

Your coach comes up and says, "You're done for the day." He doesn't sound mad. He may even sound proud.

You've played hurt. You've done what you were supposed to do.

Later, when doctors ask you to list the concussions in your life, when they are testing your brain for damage, you cite this as the third concussion. You know it is at least that. You may have forgotten some. It could be your fourth or fifth. But that would be a guess.

———

WINTER 1979: You are the only white kid, drinking with your best friends from the winter basketball league, Malcolm and Terry and a few other kids you don't know that well.

Malcolm always brings red wine. You once ask him if he could get you some beer and he laughs at you. "Tom Pitty-Patty, beer is a very fucking white thing to drink. White people drink beer and then sit around the next day talking about how much beer they drank."

You are passing the bottle and you and Terry are sharing a Swisher Sweet and snow is falling in soft heavy flakes that look as big as packing peanuts.

Someone complains that he'll have to shovel that fucking snow in the morning. One of the guys says that Super John Williamson won't have to shovel *his* snow.

Super John Williamson is a hero of all of yours. He plays for the New Jersey Nets. He's from the poorest, worst part of New Haven and it's a famous story in local basketball circles that as a kid, Super John Williamson had to shovel snow just to help his family get enough money to eat.

He was truly poor and you feel guilty, sitting around with guys like Malcolm and Terry, who are also poor, while you live two towns over and you're fine. Your parents are solidly middle class and you are white and even at thirteen you know you have an enormous and unfair advantage.

Super John Williamson shoveled snow from the time he was seven years old and he knew what it felt like to go to bed hungry and he dreamed about getting the fuck out of shitty New Haven and he did because he was one of the greatest basketball players anyone had ever seen.

Super John Williamson vowed that when he made it, he would buy his mother a house and he would build himself a mansion and he would never shovel snow again.

And now, everybody around knows that Super John Williamson signed a huge contract with the Nets and has a mansion in New Haven that has heating coils installed under the driveway, so that when it snows, he flicks a switch and the snow fucking *melts* and he's done interviews about how he flicks that switch and he watches his snow melt and he remembers every shovel full of snow he ever had to lift.

Super John Williamson has even, you're pretty sure, had his name legally changed from his given name to his nickname. He was just John Williamson, but now he's Super John Williamson and everyone has to call him that.

He is the essence of cool to all of you. He is a sign of where basketball can take you.

Every single one of you on these steps thinks he is going to be a pro basketball player. You and six million other kids are convinced they'll be one of the three hundred NBA players.

You're all getting a little buzzed from the wine and someone says you should go watch the snow melt at Super John Williamson's house.

Seven of you pile into Malcolm's brother's car. None of you are old enough to drive. Malcolm is the oldest, at fifteen, but he shouldn't be driving—maybe more than any of you. He's been arrested at least twice for stealing and joyriding in stranger's cars. With these priors, he could be arrested and locked up for driving his brother's car. If you or Terry were driving, or any of the other guys, you'd be arrested, but it probably wouldn't mean you'd be locked up. But you can't drive and even if you could, you'd never take the risk. You are the smallest person in the car, so you sit on the center console between the two front seats, facing backward with your ass aching the whole way.

The snow starts sticking to the road on Route 95 and it's slick by the time you get to the house. You park across the street. The seven of you spill out of the car. The snow is falling more quickly now and you stand across the street, and you all watch in awe as the streets and sidewalks grow thick and white with snow and Super John Williamson's driveway sits, black and wet and warm.

You think you see someone look out at you from inside the house, but you can't be sure if this is memory or invention.

In three years, Malcolm will be dead—thrown off the roof of a six-story building in Bridgeport. Terry will be in a wheelchair, a quadriplegic from a gunshot to the neck. You are the only one who ever leaves his hometown. Even Super John Williamson will owe so much in back taxes to the IRS, he will one day lose the glorious house you are staring at in the falling snow.

7

1920S AND 1930S: Johnny Eck, the amazing "Half-Boy" and "King of the Freaks," performs in several sideshows, becoming most famous for his role as the Half Boy in Tod Browning's 1932 cult classic, *Freaks*.

Eck is born in 1911 with just over half a body due to sacral agenesis. He has unusable, underdeveloped legs and feet that he later hides under custom-made clothing. At birth, Eck weighs two pounds and is not even eight inches long. He grows to be eighteen inches tall. He has a fully bodied fraternal twin, Robert—though the two look remarkably alike and exploit this throughout their sideshow careers.

In 1937 Eck and Robert join the "Miracles of 1937" show. In it, they perform probably the greatest variation ever on the classic illusion of a magician sawing a person in half. When the magician asks for a volunteer, Robert stands and goes to the stage and gets in the box, preparing to be cut in half. During the trick, Robert is replaced by his brother in one side of the box and a dwarf wearing pants that come up over his head in the other side. When the halves are separated, Robert's "legs" jump out of the box and run away—often up the aisle of the theater. Eck then jumps from his half of the box, propelling himself with his hands, shouting for his legs to stop and come back.

A woman is hired who sits in the front row and can projectile vomit at will. Every night, while Eck chases his legs, she stands, vomits, and pretends to faint. The act plays to sold-out houses.

1990: You are living in Sarasota. You can't remember if you are unemployed at this point or not, but you know that you have become increasingly erratic and need at least three beers every morning to stop shaking. You and Mary are still a couple but no longer live together—her roommates never agreed to live with you, and you move out to avoid the uncomfortable situation.

You live in what used to be a motel on Route 41, but it's been turned into apartments by some slumlord. Your unit is across from what used to be the complex's pool, but is now an empty, cracked, kidney-bean-shaped concrete hole filled with rancid water from the summer rains, which grows a sickly, freakish neon green with algae. There are an astounding number of mosquitoes at night. Somehow frogs manage to survive in the muck at the bottom of the pool.

Your neighbor and good friend on the other side of what used to be the pool is a guy named Dan—this causes some problems, as your roommate and Dan's roommate are also named Dan. Collectively they are known as, understandably, "the Dans." But when you need to refer to them individually, your good friend is Tat Dan (because he's a tattoo artist), his roommate is Big Dan (because he's six foot eight), and your roommate, who never pays rent and wracks up outrageous phone charges to Puerto Rico under your name, is known as Broke Dan.

One night, Tat Dan gets an offer to do some work at Showtown, a bar in Gibsonton, known as Gibtown to locals. The whole trailer-park town is the off-season/retirement community for sideshow freaks. They don't like going out in public, so Dan will do their tats at the bar. The residents of Gibtown are famous for disliking outsiders and for hyperaggressively trying to keep them away. But Dan knows you love sideshows—you have always been fascinated with people who don't fit in some fundamental way—so he sells them on the story that you are his assistant and learning how to become a tattoo artist yourself. He convinces them that you are somehow necessary.

So you end up being one of the rare outsiders who gets to go to Showtown. You are hoping, above all, to meet Grady Stiles Jr., Lobster Boy. You do not know it at this point—you find out later from the articles about his murder—but he rarely drinks at the bar, electing to spend most of his nights watching TV in his trailer, drinking and chain-smoking Pall Malls.

Tat Dan is doing some touch-up work on a strongman who looks just like the most stereotypical strongman you can imagine—you can easily see him lifting weights that have black balls at the ends of the barbell. He has a handlebar mustache that reminds you of Greg Norton from Hüsker Dü. Or Rollie Fingers. You are aware of very few other men with handlebar mustaches.

After standing around for a while not doing much of anything, you worry that it will become apparent that you are not Dan's assistant but some outsider gawking at these people for no good reason. They get gawked at all the time, sure. They're used to it. But that's their profession. That's their day job—and who wants to do their job when they're sitting around having a few drinks and trying to relax? You are a little sick with yourself. These are human beings. They don't exist so that you can look at them and see how different they are from you. In fact, you tell yourself, this is a moment to realize that *you* exist to understand that the sideshows aren't different from you and deserve more respect than you had when you said yes to coming to Showtown. Than when you walked in the door and lied to them about what you were doing there.

From overhearing a conversation at the bar over the intermittent buzz of Tat Dan's gun, you understand that the barback has not shown up and the bartender's doing double duty clearing and cleaning glasses and getting liquor from the back room. You volunteer to help. After looking at you for a moment, the bartender decides to take you on. There is nothing visibly different about this man and you guess

that he might be one of the barkers. He could be a magician. He could run rides. The majority of the sideshow isn't
the freaks, after all.

You work your ass off, trying to prove that you're not
there for the wrong reasons, even though, really, you are.
Later, your barback duties finished, you are having a pleasant conversation about the funding of Social Security with
the World's Smallest Woman and the Alligator Man. They
have been married to each other for decades. And then,
you can't help yourself. While he's talking, you look at the
scaly skin on his forearms instead of maintaining eye con-
tact. You look at the skin on his neck while you should be
looking at his wife when she's talking. His skin looks like
dead fish you've seen, washed up on the shore and gray in
the sunlight, their scales flaking away in the breeze.

He catches you looking at him and you look away, feeling ashamed that you are no different from anybody else
who paid their money to go look at the freak.

2012: You are at a rest stop in California off the I-10 freeway. You are in a manic episode—but not yet a dangerous
one. It's one of the good ones, like your brain is a thousand
Fourth of July sparklers and everything is in high focus
and life is beautiful. You write your best friend, Gina, an
e-mail from your phone, your fingers moving frantically
from your mania:

> . . . *i dont care about anything bad at the moment-ha! I'm
> in a little bit of a glorious manic high that clicked in about*

4am when I couldn't sleep and I started to get the taste
of coins at the back of my tongue (a sure sign that I'm ei-
ther about to snap manic or break down) and I've felt like
so VERY aware and alive (though, yes, sick) . . . tired on
one hand but so awake in another I feel like I'd electrocute
anyone who shook my hand—it feels like my brain could
juggle chainsaws right now—and it's like my head is this in
between quiet and loud . . . well, it IS loud, but it's like it's
loud with the smallest things. Like I could stand on the road
and hear ants eating if I tried hard enough.

2011: Your brain stabilizers, which you don't dare stop
taking, cause vicious and frequent leg spasms—but only at
night. It's a common side effect of the drug. Some people's
side effects are so bad that they commit suicide. When the
spasms come on, they are like a seizure and at their worst
can last up to six hours. One night, while Gayle is away
visiting her parents, you spasm and jerk in bed so violently
that you wake up with trouble breathing and a sharp pain
in your chest. You go to the urgent care clinic, where they
do an X-ray.

The doctor comes into the room and tells you you've
torn a muscle from your rib cage. She asks you if you've
had an accident.

You feel ashamed to tell her that you did it to yourself.
You explain about the side effect of your meds.

She says, "We don't tend to see this unless someone was
in a car accident." She looks at you. "You're telling me you
did this in your sleep?"

Technically, you did it in bed. You were not asleep. You can't sleep though these episodes. You just have to wait until your body finally stops.

You say, "Yeah. Pretty much."

She offers you a script of Vicodin for the pain. You are incredibly tempted. After all, you *are* in legitimate pain. Maybe you could take them like a normal person. But, whether or not you like yourself, you do know yourself. You want the pain meds badly. And who would know? You consider your options for a moment.

"No," you tell her. And then you admit that you're an addict, which you hate, because they write it on your chart and it means you'll never get pain meds there no matter how much you beg. You've been good. But you still want the option to fuck up later, even if you know it's a mistake. You wish you hadn't told her. And then you thank her and end up popping Advil for weeks, wishing you had taken the Vicodin. Still, you brag to your friends in recovery that you turned it down. You don't tell them about your regret at having done so.

SEPTEMBER 1993: You quit drinking. One day you wake up and simply can't do it anymore. Later you'll find out at AA meetings that this is quite common. There's no big epiphany. No moment of realization. Just a quiet final awareness that you are going to die if you keep this up and, for some reason, you don't want to die. Maybe it's simply exhaustion after a decade like this, but you can't go on the way you've been going.

You make the mistake of quitting alone and after nearly twenty-four hours without a drink, you have a grand mal seizure. You should be in a hospital. You are living alone under piles of garbage in your grandmother's hoarder house—which you get to live in for free in exchange for cleaning it up. You don't call anybody that first day.

The seizure starts with an aura, a sort of buzzing, floating sensation at the base of your neck, and blue lights halo in front of your eyes. At first, it doesn't seem much different than a migraine. You feel like this has happened before. There's a mild sense of déjà vu, but you're aware enough to know you've never felt anything quite like it. You are dizzy and you sit in the chair where you read. Your tongue feels heavy and tastes like a wet metallic rag, similar to the start of a manic episode but slightly different. You become scared you are going to die but you can't get up to reach the phone.

You begin seeing things. The shadows of the leaves through the windows start to look like claws coming toward you and you are hearing voices but you can't make out words. The visual and auditory hallucinations are like a psychotic episode, but you can already tell it's not one of those. There is no feeling of any high accompanying it. Plus, your head aches, which is not normal.

You have no idea why, but you start clicking your reading light on and off. You later will find out this is a symptom of the first part of the seizure. The clock on the table reads 3:00 a.m.

You feel your body jerk and you collapse onto the floor.

It sounds like someone dropping a huge duffel bag—the sound of something falling not in stages but all at once. Your body spasms around and you have no control over it. The last thing you remember is your head repeatedly banging against the hardwood floor.

You wake up on the floor. Your arms and legs and head are sore and your elbows and knees are swollen. The clock reads 7:00 a.m.

1973: Your parents are at some party and they've dragged you along. All the adults have kids, but you don't know any of them and this terrifies you. You don't mind being alone by yourself. But you dread being alone around other people. You always have. Nothing is lonelier than being the new kid, the outsider. All the other kids are three or four or five years older than you. Important years. You're stuck as the youngest person at the party.

You will remember three facts from the party. The first fact is that the adults are upstairs and have made it very clear that the kids are supposed to stay downstairs in what the hostess calls the rumpus room. Her face reminds you of the first open casket you ever saw—she's wearing a frightening amount of makeup and you want to poke your finger into it. She dresses in a miniskirt and multipatterned halter top and insists you call her Aunt Jill, though you are not in any way related—and corpse-faced Aunt Jill makes it very clear that the kids are not allowed upstairs.

The other kids seem somehow to all know one another— whether they do or not—and this is one of the first times you experience what will become a familiar feeling over the years: being thoroughly uninvited in a social gathering. You will feel like an interruption your whole life. You begin to hate your parents for bringing you to this slice of hell. The only highlight is that you make one shot in a game of pool the other kids finally let you play after you've spent hours alone in a corner. Your chest only comes to the height of the table. You've missed every other shot you've taken, but this one travels the whole length of the table and falls and for a moment you feel, rightly or wrongly, like you've impressed the group.

Not long after this triumph, you have to piss, but you're afraid to approach any of the older kids to ask where you can find the downstairs bathroom. You wait maybe an hour—it could be longer, it could be shorter, but your bladder reaches emergency levels and you're trapped between asking the big kids about a downstairs bathroom and knowing there must be one upstairs, yet you are far too frightened to go up and break Aunt Jill's adults-only rule. You don't want to disappoint or embarrass your parents by appearing upstairs where you've been told you don't belong and are not wanted.

Finally, you can't wait anymore and decided to risk a trip upstairs. The adults will surely understand the youngest kid more than the other kids will understand you.

You make it halfway up the stairs and piss your pants. The kids all laugh as the piss stain swells in the front of your pants and the piss pools on the steps and finally begins its humiliating dripping from the open-backed stairs onto the carpeted floor. Screams of laughter fill the basement. Some kid says, "Fucking disgusting."

With the commotion, a group of parents opens the upstairs door and sees you, piss spreading through your brown corduroys—more on the right leg than the left, you will remember. The pool still at your feet. Dripping from the stairs. Your parents come down—your mother seemingly embarrassed, your father angry as hell. You will remember your right sock being soaked and making a squishing noise as you walked to the car.

You have no memory of how your parents handled this once you were alone. What you remember is being in the middle of the stairs between the upstairs and downstairs, trapped between the adults and the kids. You prefer to think they handled it with love. You can't remember, so you choose to believe what you want to believe.

1999: A Hollywood agent sees one of your plays. She corners you after the play and tells you how brilliant you are. How edgy, raw, and risky your work is. She calls your work brave. You think people who save babies from burning buildings are brave, but she's praising you and you are a sucker for praise.

She says, "Do you write screenplays?"

You have never written a screenplay. Before responding, you think briefly of lives ruined by Hollywood. About Peg Entwistle, the actress who leaped to her death from the H on the Hollywood sign in 1932. How Hollywood fucked up years of Richard Yates's life and career. You may be the only

person in Los Angeles County who has never had the slight-
est desire to write a screenplay. But you are broke. And she
likes your work. You say, "I've written a few, sure." You
have no idea how to even format one of the fucking things.

She gives you her card. "Send it to me and let's have
lunch."

You tell her you'd like to do one more "polish" draft.
Would it be cool to have lunch in a couple of weeks?

She tells you to call the office and schedule the lunch.

Writing the script is surprisingly easy—though you
will learn that selling one is not easy at all. You send it to
her three days before the lunch. Across the table at a place
you could never afford, she says, "You're the real deal," and
takes you on as a client. You never consider whether you
really want to do this. You just see getting out of your shit
job that only pays sixteen grand a year.

1986: Every Sunday morning—or whenever you wake
up, which may not actually *be* morning—you listen to Van
Morrison's *Astral Weeks*. You are hungover every morning,
but for some reason, Sundays are the only time you listen
to *Astral Weeks*. It is the perfect Sunday hangover music—
hypnotic and repetitive, complex but still easy to listen to on
repeat. If you have any coke left from the night before, you
snort a line and smoke cigarettes and drink coffee, while
Astral Weeks plays in the background. You do this every Sunday into winter. The snow falls, the streets are white at
first, and then everything grows gray, a shift from life to
death in front of you. Dull slush sits in the alley where you

enter your basement apartment on Marlboro Street. Some Sundays, you play your guitar, which may or may not still have all six strings left after the night before. Every Sunday, you listen to Van Morrison.

MARCH 6, 2010: Mark Linkous, leader of the band Sparklehorse, commits suicide by shooting himself in the chest in Knoxville, Tennessee.

In 1996, while opening for Radiohead, Linkous passes out on a combination of antidepressants, Valium, and alcohol in a hotel room bathroom. He is left unconscious with his legs pinned under him for more than twelve hours, cutting off circulation. His heart stops for several minutes after he is lifted up. He nearly loses the use of both legs and is in a wheelchair for six months, never regaining total functional use of his legs. He releases a series of critically acclaimed albums before his suicide in 2010. He is forty-seven.

2012: In Chicago, during an August rainstorm, you cut three deep lines into your forearm, drawing enough blood that it runs down your arm, onto your hands, and pools on the sidewalk as it drips off your fingers.

It happens this way. Your wife is sick in a hotel room—too sick to walk around Chicago while you wait eight hours for your flight out of O'Hare. Gina had dropped you at the hotel the night before. You and Gayle made plans to check out at eleven, leave the luggage at the hotel, and hang around Chicago all day. But by ten in the morning, it's clear your wife is not going to make that eleven o'clock check-out. This angers you—and you immediately hate yourself for being angry. But then, you still resent that this keeps happening and you are angry and guilty and miserable all the same. You hate being late and she's always late. You have to remind yourself that she's sick—in pain all the time. A pain you can only imagine. Gayle is so debilitated that you doubt she'll even make a noon checkout if you extend the reservation, so you go to the desk and book another day. You see that it just cost you $188 because she can't do this basic, simple thing and be ready on time. And then you feel like an asshole again.

Rain starts to pour, but you need to get out of the room. Away from your wife, because even though you don't like being angry with her and you know none of this is her fault, you *are* angry. Away from your guilt, because who the fuck are you—the man who robbed her of her pain medication for months during your relapse—to judge her in any fucking way?

You have lost your phone charger, which becomes the perfect excuse to get away, so you go out in the rain to find a phone store. On the way to the mobile-phone place, you pass three bars. You want a drink. It hasn't been this bad in a while. You want what you chased for so many years—you want your brain to feel differently than it feels right now. You feel trapped by yourself and want out, badly. You buy the charger and deliberately walk back the same way to pass the three bars again.

The hotel also has a bar on the ground floor. You look

in the window, taking shelter from the rain under a small awning. You are soaked though and your glasses are wet and fogged and when you try to dry them on your shirttail you smudge water all over them.

You think for a while about going into the bar. It's not like there's even that much time before the flight. And you couldn't let Gayle see you drunk, so you are thinking two, maybe three drinks at the most. How good they would feel after so long. The veil of calm that would fall over you. The nerves untangling. Your messy head clearing and quieting. Everything you miss.

You see a shattered bottle of Heineken on the sidewalk, some of the glass slivers still held next to each other by the label's adhesive backing. You pick up one piece of glass that's shaped like a slice of pizza. You thinking about walking in the bar and you try to fight it, but you need to change the way you feel somehow. You roll up your wet sleeve. You cut your forearm, deep but not enough for stitches. The three lines swell with blood and immediately you relax and look in the bar and realize you don't need a drink. The blood mixes with little puddles of rainwater, looking like red squid ink as it spreads and thins.

You roll down your sleeve and go up to your room and charge your phone. A week later you will tell Gina, no one else. Your wife will never know. Never know how close you came to drinking again. You will never mention it to your sponsor or share it at a meeting. You think: *It stopped me. Whose business is it, then?*

1986: You're back from Holland and you're managing a Häagen-Dazs in Boston on Charles Street.

It's a slow, unseasonably cold spring night, but it was warmer when you started your shift and you are wearing cargo shorts. Dire Straits is on the radio. "Telegraph Road."

You could send your co-worker Brenda home. You should have. You have a crush on her and this is a time in your life when you will sleep with pretty much any attractive woman who is willing to sleep with you. You've discovered in the last year or so that you love sex, and you also love variety. On the other hand—and this will make you cringe for years after the fact—in pursuit of both you are also racking up women like trophies. Part of this impulse comes from being so afraid you're not attractive that you need constant confirmation you are. The other part, you think, sadly, is that you're kind of a scumbag.

You should let Brenda punch out. There's no reason for two of you to be there—there hasn't been a customer in at least thirty minutes and it's nine o'clock and you're only an hour before closing. By rights, your boss wouldn't even blame *you* if you decided to close early. He's probably paying the two of you more than he'll make in the next hour.

But you aren't thinking of any of this. You are thinking about an hour alone with Brenda when a man with a leather jacket over a gray hooded sweatshirt rushes into the door and points a gun first at you, then Brenda, then back to you and tells you to open the register. Brenda—not you, you will always remember—is smart enough to say, "We're looking down. At your shoes. We haven't seen your face."

You punch the register open and he takes everything.

"The safe," he says.

You're unable to move. You feel like someone's choking you. You can't talk. Only the owner knows the combo to the safe. It has a drop slot for the white envelopes you fill with cash when there's too much money in the till.

He screams, "The safe!"

You manage to tell him that neither of you has the combination.

"Bullshit."

Brenda says, "He's telling the truth. We just drop the money in."

He points the gun at your head. You are looking down at his thighs, but you can still tell where his left arm is aiming.

He says very slowly, "What. Is. The. Fucking. Combination?"

You say, "Honest. We have no idea."

He tells both of you to get on your knees and turn around. You do. You look down at the one-inch-square tiles and think they may be the last thing you ever see. Brenda's breathing is shallow and quick next to you on your right. You smell hot fudge.

"Really," he says calmly. "I'm giving you one last chance here."

You expect to start shaking but a strange calm comes over you. Even in the best of circumstances, you are an anxiety-riddled, neurotic mess. You have to be nearly passed-out drunk to even step on a plane. You panic when you drive over bridges that they will collapse and you will drown. But in this moment, you just think, *So this is it? This is how I'm going to die.*

"We don't have the combination," you say again.

He stands there for a moment and you wonder if this is going to hurt. It will probably be fast, you think. Not even time to feel it. You wish you had sent Brenda home—you have the presence of mind to regret that.

Then, he kicks you in the back and runs out the door.

You are alive.

Your head is swirling with the whoosh that comes from holding a big conch shell up to your ear, only a hundred times louder. You will have no memory of what Brenda says. You know she's the one who calls the cops.

After what seems like a long time, but must only be a minute at most, you realize "Telegraph Road" is still playing. The song is somewhere around ten minutes, but you would have guessed the thief had been there for at least fifteen or twenty.

Minus the noise in your head, you are still calm.

The cops come. They have their own language. The guy with the gun is a "perpetrator." The gun is a "weapon." And so on. You already know this from being arrested a few times. You tell them the only thing you noticed.

"He was left-handed," you say.

You realize you might piss yourself if you stand here answering questions much longer, that you've been holding your bladder since it happened. You ask the cop if you can go to the bathroom, which is in back, behind the freezers.

When you get to the bathroom, you start to feel lightheaded and you have to sit to piss. From this position you see the faint outline of the one-inch tiles imbedded on your knees and you start to shake and you cannot, no matter what you do, stop shaking. You could have died. And now, seeing the pattern of the floor tiles pressed into your skin, you are suddenly terrified.

1987: In Boston, you overdose on a mixture of benzos and alcohol in the bedroom of some woman you met that night at a party. Earlier, you had fucked. Then you felt yourself really nodding out sitting on her floor, drinking red wine after getting loaded. She later tells you that you started to gag and then stopped breathing.

You wake up on the floor of her apartment while she is roughly shoving ice cubes up your asshole in an attempt to revive you. It works. You come to and see she's furious. You're almost certain her name is Toni. She screams at you, "I don't *know* you well enough to be sticking ice cubes in your ass!"

1989: You are near the end—but not yet, it turns out, *at* the end—of a very bad and very long run with drinking and drugs and you've decided to leave Boston for a place that seems peaceful and tranquil and where you can clean up and inch closer to sobriety. For some reason, you are convinced that trees are essential to sobriety. Clearly it's the city that isn't working, not the booze or the drugs or you. Time for a move.

You choose Humboldt County.

You have no idea that Humboldt is known for anything, let alone great pot, as pot is not your drug of choice and you don't even hang out much with people who smoke it. When a joint or bong is passed at a party, you take a hit, but you really have no idea if you even like pot, since you've never tried it unless you already have four or five other drugs in your system. When people ask if you like pot, you answer, "It doesn't seem to do much to me."

You choose Humboldt almost at random. You are in your student-loan office in Boston, trying to explain why you can't pay them, when you see a brochure for Humboldt State University in Arcata, California. It has a redwood tree on the cover. A river. Lush evergreens. No drug dealers. It looks like the perfect place to clean up your act, start a new life. Even better, if you are in grad school, you can defer your undergrad loans until later. And you don't tend to worry much about "later."

You enroll at Humboldt, drive cross-country after sobering up for a week (you tapered down and your D.T.'s are nowhere near what they'll be when you finally do quit for good) and are amazed that you don't wake up puking every morning before your first coffee and cigarette. You and clean living are getting along okay. By the time you reach Lake Tahoe, you have spent more days clean in a row (eight) than in the previous five years combined. A new life awaits.

You start classes at Humboldt State University, but it's clear from the first you don't belong—in either the school or the town. You have a terrible living situation with two brothers, Don and Ron Wright. The Wright brothers, though you nickname them the Wrong brothers. They hang with meth heads and drinkers and you spend all your time at home holed up in your room, drinking coffee and working very hard not to drink anything else.

The only bright spot of those two and a half months in Arcata is that you meet Gayle. You first see her at orientation, but you don't know her name. Then you run into her at the grocery store. You jerk off thinking about her before you even know her name. When you finally do officially meet, you tell her she reminds you of Jodie Foster. She tells you she gets that a lot. You clarify, say you meant the voice, too. That she also sounds like Jodie Foster. And she tells you, yeah, she gets that a lot, too.

You don't really talk much until one day before class when you have a cigarette together. She later tells you that she'd already smoked one before class, but when she saw you, she went out to have another as an excuse to talk. It's immediately clear how smart she is. You say something that makes her laugh and you flood with happiness at the mere wonder that she might be enjoying your company. You start off as friends and quickly become close friends. You want to be with her, but she's in a long-distance relationship with this guy Mickey, who's down in Southern California. Between really enjoying your time with Gayle and the dreadful situation at your place, you end up sleeping on her couch nearly every night for a month, while she sleeps in the bed in her loft. You do end up fucking twice, but afterward, she says she's trying monogamy for the first time with Mickey, so you stop sleeping together. The first time you fuck, it starts because you are holding each other on the couch, watching the Robert Towne movie *Tequila Sunrise*, and one of you mentions how terrible it is, and a second later you are kissing.

You leave Humboldt after only two and a half months because you are already flunking out of school and you're going to have trouble staying sober, trees or no trees. You don't want her to see who you are when you drink. You and Gayle will spend more than two years talking long distance. Talking about sex and literary theory and what's going on in your lives. She's the first woman who doesn't make you feel embarrassed when you admit to submissive desires. The hours disappear without a pause in your conversations. When you are living in Amherst, you often call her at midnight and you're still on the phone when the sun comes up. Your phone bills cost more than your rent.

Before you leave Humboldt you start drinking again. Slowly and moderately at first, but a week after you start, you black out behind the wheel and drive your car into a ditch off Highway 101. You wake up at dawn surrounded by the thickest fog you have ever seen. Your car is still running. The CD player is still playing. Jonathan Richman's "Government Center." The last thing you remember is leaving a bar in Eureka. You are lucky a cop didn't see you in the ditch. You are much luckier you didn't kill someone. You shake with fear and self-hatred. You are no different from someone who *did* kill someone driving drunk. You are only luckier.

What you are capable of scares the shit out of you. And then there are the things you're not capable of right now. Like grad school. You are drinking. You know you need to get the hell out of there before you destroy the one good thing you've found at Humboldt—your friendship with Gayle.

In a stroke of what qualifies as luck at this point in your life, your grandmother Ament has died. Her house is filled with fifty years of garbage that your father has no desire to deal with. You ask him what he's going to do with all her junk.

"Burn it to the fucking ground if you can figure out a way the cops and your mother won't know," he says.

You end up cutting a deal with him where you get to live for free in your grandmother's disgusting house in exchange for cleaning it. Half a century of garbage. Ten-year-old frozen fish your long-dead grandfather had caught. Mice and rats, some dead and flattened, and their dried shit all over everything. A smell you will never forget. A series of your grandmother's cigarette burns in the wood floor from years of passing out drunk in front of her TV.

The house has only two paths: one from the back door to the fridge and another from her TV chair to the bathroom—shit piled over your head on either side as you walk and stumble along. Flies swarm like in scenes from *The Amityville Horror*. The house has a dirt-floor basement with mushrooms growing in the dirt and about fifty bird-houses your grandfather made to regain his motor skills after his stroke. You use the birdhouses as firewood. You drink the cases of odd wines he made over the years—apple wine from his orchard. Pear wine. Dandelion wine. They are all noxious. But they *are* alcohol.

The path to the fridge where you can keep the off-brand

beer and gin you can afford is already cleared for you. And you know a Percocet dealer not far away. Things, examined in a certain light, are looking up.

2000: You have just handed your film agent your fifth script in a row, which is an awful lot like the play that made her want to represent you in the first place.

"You write so indie," she tells you. "They're awfully edgy." She's behind her desk. You are across from her in a ridiculously comfortable chair. Her assistant brings you coffee. In the film business, you learn, they often treat you very well while they are treating you like shit.

Your agent says, "Everything you're giving me is a hard sell at best."

You think about how good *edgy* and *raw* once sounded coming out of her mouth. "Well, I mean . . . this is kind of what I do," you say. "What I write." You want to ask her why she took you on as a client if your voice was a "hard sell." Your dreams of money are shriveling the more she speaks. You think you'll be stuck at your shitty job editing technical manuals forever.

"I thought you'd have found more of the formula by now." She has, since your second script, been giving you scripts of produced movies to review as reference for your own material. Some are things you think you might be able to write. Most are for movies where aliens invade and blow the absolute shit out of everything on the planet before they lose their war with humanity. You have nothing against those movies, but it's obvious that you have to love movies where shit blows up if you are going to write a good movie where shit blows up. It's just not you.

You say, "I thought you liked my play."

"Oh, honey. I still want to work with you, but you need to start thinking differently."

You sit closer to the edge of the comfortable chair. Even before you say it, you hate yourself, call yourself a chicken-shit whore, but you still ask, "How should I think?"

She sighs. "What you need to ask yourself is, What would Ed Norton look cool doing for two hours?" She leans forward and claps once. "And write that."

You think Ed Norton would look plenty cool in your indie, edgy, raw hard sells. You don't say anything.

Your agent, though you already sense that you will not be calling her that after you walk out the door today, says, "Okay. Let's look at it this way. Let's say you're the hottest new shit on the block. You just came out of Sundance with your first film and everyone's dying for a piece of you. You can call whatever shot you want. Make any movie you choose." She pauses. "What's your dream project?"

You say, "The Johnny Eck story."

She asks who Johnny Eck is and you tell her.

"Pick another one," she says.

"The Lobster Boy story."

"What the fuck is that?" she says. It's the first time ever that she hasn't sounded gentle and condescendingly kind.

You tell her the Lobster Boy story.

She shakes her head. "What actor is going to want to play a lobster? A fucking half man?"

"Johnny Depp," you say.

"Fine," she says. "Where do we go when Johnny Depp says no?"

"Johnny Depp won't say no," you tell her.

This is your last day with a film agent. You have decided that you have written your last script. Or perhaps everyone else decided that for you.

2004: You are teaching at the UCLA Extension Writers' Program, which can attract some crazy people. Generally, you like crazy people. You are a crazy person. Doctors have tagged the label on you more than once. You've grabbed the bus at the stop closest to the hospital, having forgotten to take off your seventy-two-hour observational plastic wristband ID.

One of your students is Karl, who has worked in several cities in Europe. He tells you he was a coke-dealing bartender in Copenhagen, where he brags of logging a Mick Jagger–esque number of sexual conquests over the years. He was later a coke-dealing bartender in a hip joint in Paris, with the same results. You listen. You're no one to judge in such matters. He seems almost like a parody of the person you used to be, and you feel bad for him.

The first night of class, he arrives before anyone else, about six foot four, middle-aged, a very good-looking, if weathered, guy. He looks like someone who'd be chain-smoking in a Truffaut film with Jeanne Moreau. He'd be much more attractive if not for the absurd leather pants (black, which is fine, piped with bright red, which is not), leather jacket, and an M&M red motorcycle helmet that loudly announces his refusal to age gracefully.

Poking you in the chest, he announces in some vague European accent: "I drove a Ducati across the fucking country to work with you!"

You've published a few stories in some literary journals, but only one has appeared online, and is therefore the most widely distributed of your work. So, you figure, maybe he's read that story, or—even weirder and better—this guy has tracked down and read and loved all your stories in obscure literary magazines.

You bask in the glory of this moment. You mentally forgive him the poke in the chest. You replay his vague, European voice in your head: *I drove a Ducati across the fucking country to work with you!*

"Really?" you say.

He waves dismissively. "You, or someone like you."

The class filters in. Eight out of the nine other people in the workshop are women. Normally you might not notice this, but—right away—it's clear that Karl is not just creepy but creepy in a very male way. The vibe in the class is unusually tense from the get-go. Everyone, except for the one other guy, seems uneasy around Karl.

The class is structured so that each student has their work critiqued by the class once or twice. But, as the professor, you read and comment on every piece they write. You have them write one story a week. Karl has signed up to be critiqued just once—the ninth week—so you are the only one to have seen his writing.

Every single one of Karl's stories is a first-person narrative about a guy who has bounced around several European cities. Who was a coke-dealing bartender in Copenhagen. Who drove a Ducati and wore leather pants.

This Karl-esque narrator, though, has another enduring trait that never fails to show up on the page: He wants to fuck his brother's fourteen-year-old daughter. In every story the narrator visits his brother in Paris and finds creepy ways to be around his niece and, when his niece is not there, he—again, in every story—slinks into her room and goes through her things and sniffs her panties.

It is difficult to read this week after week. You wish you had his brother's phone number. But it is a writing class—a creative exercise—and you wouldn't, ugly as the work is, want to censor a writer's material. You approach Karl's work with caution, offering some praise but pointing out the whole niece thing could really offend readers. You hope to get through to Karl more about what he might be doing than about what he's writing.

Week nine arrives. The class where Karl's work is discussed.

Even before the class starts, the ashen faces of the other students—who have read Karl's story in preparation—let you know you're in for a tough night. Three women haven't shown up. The rest look either angry or shell-shocked. You extend the banter at the start of class as long as you can—delay tactics that eventually stall out because no one is in the mood for playful small talk.

It's finally time to talk about Karl's story. No one has

a response. Usually you try to get class started by getting out of the way a little—letting the students set the tone for the discussion and only starting to jump in (and, as is your manic habit, rarely shut up) about halfway into a critique, unless there's an issue of craft or a total lull in the room. And this sort of silence is starting to make that "total lull" seem positively raucous.

You don't have many rules in class. You try to be descriptive, rather than prescriptive, when you work with writers. But there is one rule: With any first-person narrative, the group is not to mistake the author for the narrator. There are important reasons for this rule—narrative persona and the author NOT being the same. Issues of biographical criticism are problematic for workshops, especially fiction workshops, where some writers want the privacy that fiction affords. And a bunch of other reasons influenced both by a concern for people's feelings and by narrative theory.

So for instance, you ask them to say "On page seven, when the narrator goes to Trader Joe's" instead of "On page seven, when you go to Trader Joe's." And so on.

Finally, a very brave and understandably troubled young writer speaks. She's maybe twenty-five and frighteningly talented—you hope the class doesn't scar her and cost the world a fine writer.

She says, "On page three, where the narrator . . . uhmm. Well, where the narrator . . . well, when the narrator's brother and sister-in-law . . . well, the whole family, really, are gone . . . the narrator goes into his niece's room and . . ." She pauses for a very long time. "Well, I guess I'm trying to say I was troubled when the narrator . . . went into his niece's room and . . . well, sniffed her underwear."

Karl looks over at her, then around the circle, smiling widely. He waves up and down and then starts pounding on the table and shouts, "THAT IS ME!"

No one speaks. You try to save the situation. To turn this into a "teachable moment" or something.

You say you agree with the student. "How about anyone else? Did any other readers feel troubled by that scene?"

Arms shoot up.

Karl says, "You don't understand what is happening? I am sniffing her panties!"

"No," you say. "We're following the action. We understand what is happening in the story." You go on to explain that a forty-year-old uncle making a trip to his brother's house solely for the purpose of trying to fuck his fourteen-year-old niece might, well, offend readers. And that the panty-sniffing scene is pretty much in the same boat, as scenes go. That the reader might be so offended that they wouldn't read a word beyond that scene.

You start to talk about other narratives that assault their audience's sensibilities—by writers who, of course, *meant* to assault their audience's sensibilities. You hope this part, at least, might be useful to the rest of the class.

Karl says, "What the fuck is fucking offensive here?"

Another student says, "I'm not going to dignify this story by talking about it."

It strikes you that not only is she right but she should probably be running the class.

You look around at the blank faces. "Why don't we take a break?"

After the break, you are down to only four students. You send people home early, more exhausted by that one hour than any full four-hour class you've ever taught. You sprint to a bathroom on the other side of the building and hide for fifteen minutes at an alternate exit in hopes that Karl is not waiting to talk with you. You make it to your car safely, and you tell yourself, over and over, that there is only one week in the semester left.

The last night of class, it's just you, Karl, and the other guy.

After you call the class early, Karl grabs his motorcycle helmet and says, "So how do I get a fucking script sold? I could take these stories and make them like *Die Hard*."

You think about a *Die Hard* with Bruce Willis as an incestuous panty-sniffing pedophile. "You'd have to take a screenwriting class. I have no idea how to sell scripts."

You make some awkward comment about getting back to your car and you start walking.

Karl asks if you want a smoke. You tell him thanks, but you quit.

A drink?

Sadly, the same answer.

"I have some blow that will keep us up until next week."

The thought of "us" being up until next week scares you much more than the idea of getting high for the first time in a decade.

You don't get offered drugs much anymore. And he's not

someone you want to be huddled on a couch over a table with but, still, you're glad he hasn't tested your not-so-iron-at-times will with, say, morphine. If something more appealing were offered in a moment of your weakness, who knows? Any good opiate could have you dumb enough to ride cross-country with Karl if he kept you stocked. You say, "I wish I could, but I can't do that anymore."

"It's Merck. You ever had it?"

Merck cocaine. A dentist across from one of your apartments in Boston used to sell it to you and your roommates, along with a tank of nitrous oxide that got replaced with a new full tank every week. Pharmaceutical-grade cocaine that could make even an opiate addict who didn't like uppers salivate. Clean, incredibly good cocaine, with no speed cut in so you wouldn't chew your gums for ten hours. Fluffy like the way heaven's clouds are depicted in children's books.

"Thanks," you say. "I'd love to, Karl. But those days are over."

"Your fucking wife, right?"

This is not the reason. Though you can't imagine Gayle would be too happy to hear you were on a weeklong blow bender with the panty-sniffing guy you've been telling her about for nine weeks. Gayle didn't really know the old you. She's never, for instance, had to bail you out of jail. Or take you to the hospital. She hasn't seen you actually hang out with a guy like Karl just because he had drugs.

You realize you miss drugs a lot more than you miss who and what you used to be when you were on them.

Both of you stand there a while longer with, clearly, nothing left to say. You are so quiet that you're sure if you were still in the classroom, you could hear the click of the second hand on the clock. Karl seems sad in a way you feel somehow responsible for, though you have no idea what you could or should have done. Part of you—a large part— thinks, *Fuck him. He's a truly disgusting creep who fucked up the class.* A small part of you thinks, *Well, he's still human and he seems so raw in his need for company tonight, it hurts to be around him.*

But he just nods and starts toward his ridiculous red mo- torcycle. You watch him walk away until his black leathers and the dark night blend.

You stand in the empty lot, feeling like a failure. Every good writer and every good person in the class had been scared off and it was your job to create a space where that wouldn't happen. Still, you had no idea what to do, then or now, with Karl.

Him, or someone like him, at any rate.

8

1977: In fourth-grade science class, where you are Nicole's "science buddy," there are two white rats named Starsky and Hutch. You will never remember what they were for— probably some horrible tests a fourth grader should never be allowed to perform. You will wonder if she ever told you, though you will remember for years the two of you holding one rat each and then putting them back on urine-soaked wood chips in their filthy cage. After you put them back, it is another pair's turn to hold them. You have no idea what happened to those rats. Were they still alive that last day of school, June 23, the day after Nicole's murder, the day of cop cars escorting all the school buses, the day very little tends to get done anyway but the day you will only ever remember as the day you heard about the murder on the radio. You will remember the cop car. You remember her empty seat. You remember the science teacher,

Mr. Karr, openly weeping. You will remember the school's floors already buffed and shined, ready for summer break.

2013: Scientists estimate that human language will survive human beings for only two to three generations of parrots. The last human words ever spoken will not be spoken by people but probably by a third-generation parrot following the extinction of human beings. Many linguists identify "becos," meaning "bread," as the first word spoken by the human race. No one will know what the last word will be. But we know it will happen thirty to fifty years after we are gone.

1981: You are at a keg party at some rich kid's house when his parents are out of town. You know his parents. You wait on them at the country club on the other side of town. His father treats you like shit.

After breaking a lamp in the master bedroom, you steal a handful of pills from his parents' bathroom—you have no idea what they are, so you start with only two, a responsible and moderate decision—a blue one and an orange-ish one you will come to know well. Valium. In the living room, someone hands you a guitar. You play the intro to the Who's "Substitute." It's a three-chord intro, and you play it twice and Karen Lewis starts making out with you. You're in the school band together and you've had a crush on her since the start of the year, although she's never seemed to notice you before this.

In band, you play the oboe. No one has ever, not once,

made out with you after you played the oboe for fifteen seconds. Guitar players, you realize, don't have to talk much. They can play someone else's music and sing someone else's song and everyone acts like they've created something. Karen Lewis grabs your crotch hard through your jeans while biting your lower lip. You wonder why anyone plays the fucking oboe.

1990: You read an interview with a dominatrix in one of Broke Dan's underground zines. You had no idea there was such a thing as a dominatrix. In the interview she talks about beating a man's ass. You are alone. Dan's in Puerto Rico visiting his girlfriend. You want to know how this feels. You close the shades and the apartment goes dark. You strip and try to find something to hit yourself with and end up using one of his thick artist's brushes. You're on your hands and knees, and you reach behind and swing the thick wood of the brush against your ass as hard as you can. At first, there's nothing but pain. Then you feel the heat on your skin and the tightness from the welts you are raising. You do this for more than ten minutes. Until there's no pain at all—just heat and calm with every swing. You wish you could ask Mary for this, but you are afraid. You stop and jerk off. Afterward, you lie naked on your couch, your ass sore and tingling, watching dust specks float in the sunlight let in through a crack in the blinds, feeling as lonely as you can remember ever feeling.

———

1991: You and Mary are still together, but you don't live together and you rarely fuck anymore. One night, you are drunk and you finally get the courage up to ask her to tie you down and hit you. To your horror, she doesn't even answer. You were braced for a possible no—though that would have been devastating. This is worse, though. She changes the subject and you both get another drink. You feel a fire of shame somewhere in your core. You think you've just guaranteed that she will leave you. And you have been close for so long. You don't know how you will face a world where you've been rejected by Mary, the person who knows you best. The person who now knows you just a little better and didn't seem to like what she learned.

1975: You are nine years old. You have saved your money from allowance and mowing lawns and harvesting potatoes at Johnson's Farm, and you have purchased Bruce Springsteen's *Born to Run* at the Sam Goody at the mall.

You look at the cover. Bruce Springsteen is cool. He's got a guitar. Guitar players are cool—even at nine years old you know that much. Your dad, who's a narcotics officer, says Springsteen's dressed like a homeless fucking hippie. By nine, you have already decided where "homeless fucking hippie" falls in relation to "narcotics officer" on the bell graph of cool.

You take the album out of its plastic. You look at the sleeve, checking both sides. You see that Springsteen, on the front cover, is leaning on a chunky black guy you later find out is Clarence Clemons, his sax player.

You put the album on. Your sister—two years older and,

therefore, cooler than you—accuses you of going "straight to the hit." She means that you've ignored the track listing and done what you always do, which is go straight to the song you know and love from the radio. Which is true. You are guilty of this. But this time, the hit, the title track, just happens to be the first cut on side *two* of the album. So she's right. You did go straight to the hit, but you lie to your sister: "No! I started it on the first song. I didn't go straight to the hit."

She says, "You would have gone to it first if it was the third song."

She is correct. You would have.

Later, while the sax solo on "Jungleland" plays, your dad walks through the room, where you sit cross-legged, listening to the album for the third time through as loud as your mother will allow. He stops for a second, listening. He says, "This guy's sax player sounds like a cross between King Curtis and Duane Eddy's sax player."

You have no idea what he's talking about. "I don't think so," you say, convinced that your narc father couldn't possibly know anything about rock and roll.

He goes downstairs, grabs *Have 'Twangy' Guitar Will Travel* by Duane Eddy and some record by "King Curtis and His All-Stars."

"Listen," he says, handing you the vinyl. "This guy sounds just like them."

You don't want to give your dad, the narc, the satisfaction. But later, while he's working on a car down in the garage, you put on this King Curtis. Your father, you hate to admit, is right. Cool Bruce Springsteen's sax player sounds a *lot* like someone in your father's record collection. This seems wrong.

Then you put on "Rebel Rouser" by Duane Eddy. It's one of the greatest sounds you've ever heard. How the hell does your dad know about this?

Your parents, you will realize much later, actually have pretty good taste in music—especially compared to your friends' Perry Como– and Pat Boone–loving parents. Yours have a lot of Ray Charles, Bob Dylan, Phil Ochs, Eric Anderson, and a bunch of great comedy albums as well.

Plus, they have all of Carly Simon's albums. You don't listen to these, but you jerk off while looking at the covers several times a day, whenever possible. *No Secrets* and *Playing Possum* being recurrent favorites.

1986: You have given two blow jobs in your life. The first was purely out of curiosity. You wanted to know what it was like. And it was, if not something you really wanted to repeat, interesting. You think cocks are pretty interesting. You think they would be a lot more interesting if they were attached to women.

The second blow job is because you feel guilty. Some law student at a party keeps giving you cocaine all night long. You have no idea that he may be hitting on you. You're just thrilled he's giving you free coke.

Later, he offers to get you a cab home. You are broke. It's five degrees out and you don't even have enough money for the T. You accept the ride, and in the back of the cab he tries to make out with you. You are uncomfortable and aren't sure what the best manners are in this situation. You don't want to kiss this man. But you feel guilty. He's been filling you with coke all night. You feel like you've violated some social contract. Like you were some tease and you didn't know it. You go down on him because sucking his cock seems a lot less intimate than actually having to kiss him.

1986: You are at the free clinic in Boston. Your cock is leaking something that looks vaguely like tartar sauce and it feels like your urethra is itchy at its core and you can't reach it. You're worried you could have something serious. You could die. Hell, other people are dying.

"Would you prefer a male doctor or a female doctor?"

You say, "Whichever."

The woman says, "It's four hours to see a male doctor. A female doctor can see you now."

The doctor sees you. After a few minutes, she tells you that you have chlamydia and she starts writing you a script.

You say, "So this goes away, right?"

"Yes," she says.

You let out a deep breath and say, "Great. Thank you so much."

She looks down and shakes her head. She says, "I remember when this was bad news."

1990: You have a scar under your left eye—about a centimeter long and straight. You do this to yourself one night when you are very drunk. You take the lid from a can you have opened and hold it at the top of your cheekbone, just underneath your eye socket. You push it hard into your face until you feel its pressure on the bone and you slice open the skin covering your cheekbone.

The next day people see the dried blood under your left eye. Naturally, they ask what happened.

You say, "I was drunk. I don't even remember."

The first part is, of course, accurate. You're always drunk, though. The second part, your lie, you wish were true. You do remember what you did. You always will. You just won't understand why you did it.

1992: You and Mary break up.

You have been best friends for a decade. You've been sleeping together for maybe eight of those years. You've been a couple, on and off, for three years.

And now it's over.

She tells you she's worried about you alone. "The world just hits you full in the face every day," she says.

You will remember being so moved that she is worried about you and not about herself when you break up. Though, objectively, just about anyone would be more worried about you than they would be about Mary. You are a mess.

1984–1988: Michelle Easter is indirectly responsible for your whole career. You meet her when you are both acting and movement majors. She's an ex-dancer who wears men's Levi's button-fly jeans rolled over low on her hips and wifebeaters and she has the first pierced nipples you've ever seen—even if you only see them through the wife-beaters. If Audrey Hepburn shaved her head and looked like you should never, ever fuck with her, she might have looked like Michelle Easter. You are smitten. She, at best, doesn't seem to be. You get it in your head, though, that with enough exposure, she will come to realize that you are a sweet, damaged young man who is a little, or a lot, lost in the world.

In the middle of freshman year, Michelle transfers from acting and movement to tech theater. So do you. She ends up designing sets. You crawl through with grades barely good enough to keep your financial aid. You spend sopho-more year in Holland, saving you the trouble of transferring into whatever Michelle transferred into that year. Junior year, Michelle takes poetry. You do too, and discover you are truly one of the most dreadful twenty-year-old poets in the history of the form. Michelle gets As and the professor tells her she's brilliant. His only critique of your work is to ask you in front of the class, every single week, "What makes you think *this* is a poem?"

You love this poet—he's a genius. It stings how much he seems to dislike you and your work. Late in the term he asks you again what makes you think what you've written is a poem.

You may like him as a poet, but you hate him as a per-son. "I don't know. It's all skinny and on the left?"

You think you might die of stunned pleasure when Michelle Easter cracks up. You go out for drinks and she repeats *It's all skinny and on the left* while laughing. You could, you think, spend a large part of your energy on this planet making Michelle Easter laugh.

Often, while you follow Michelle Easter from major to major, you are dating women who have no idea you are following Michelle Easter in her academic sampling of everything your school has to offer. You think a lot about trying to be a better person. You do very little to become one. At the time, you would have used the word *romantic* to describe your attempt to win Michelle's affections. Later, you will realize there is a more accurate word and legal term for what you were doing: stalking.

Michelle transfers to journalism. This you're good at. Except you invent every news story you report.

"You can't just make shit up," your editor tells you.

Michelle, who must realize by now that you are somehow ending up in every one of her classes, becomes a creative writing major. You are finally in a room for a better reason than following Michelle Easter around.

1992: After your breakup with Mary, you move back to your grandmother's old hoarder house, which is still not totally cleaned out, even years after her death. You could and should have done more, but you *have* hauled more than a thousand pounds of her garbage to the dump and the house still looks pretty much the same.

1980: You are finally old enough to be left home when your parents go to a party some friends are throwing. Your sister is sixteen and out with her boyfriend. You get drunk on your parents' liquor. They never notice. Your father never drinks hard liquor and your mother drinks disgustingly sweet Rhine wine every night. Your father buys his Marlboro Reds by the carton, so you take a pack and chain-smoke. You take out your grandfather's fishing tackle box. You tie his heaviest fishing line around your balls and hang a series of eight- and sixteen-ounce weights from the fishing line until it hurts. Then you jerk off. You have no idea that what you're doing is strange, or why you're doing it—you only know that it feels good.

1983: After eight minutes of agony during his botched execution in a Mississippi gas chamber, struggling to breathe, in obvious and dreadful pain, Jimmy Gray kills himself by repeatedly smashing his head into a pole behind the chair he is strapped to.

1990: In Florida, you are in the middle of a psychotic episode and you become convinced that you and only you have a plan to end all the world's suffering and you need to get the message to the president immediately.

This profound message, of course, is lost now. There is no chance it *was* a plan, let alone a good one. And there is no chance that you could have ever reached the president of the local Knights of Columbus, let alone of the United States.

Your roommates try to talk you down. But, no. You know, you just *know* that you have come up with a plan to end the world's suffering and only you can articulate it and you need to reach the most powerful person in the world and then you will have saved everyone.

You will be a hero. Your roommates are still trying to talk to you and you end up running out of your apartment. You're barefoot, wearing only jeans. It's August and Florida is soupy. Old people and babies drop dead on nights like this. Sweat stings your eyes. You must stay focused on getting to the president with your message. There's a police car turning toward you and you're on red alert. You are in a psychotic episode, but even in these states you never, never, never lose sight of what cops and hospital people can do to you. You duck around a corner and pray they didn't see you. Just being out without a shirt and shoes can get you a curb sit and they will not understand what you have to say to the president and they will lock you up. Once you turn that corner, veer off track, you keep going and you end up walking five miles south to a beach, looking over your shoulder the whole way.

Your feet are cut—there are bits of crushed windshield glass stuck in your skin—and it hurts to walk. You are still in the episode, but you no longer believe you've got this plan to save the world. You just know now that you must have *had* a psychotic episode, because of how different they feel from waking up from a blackout. Waking up from a blackout, you need to puke. The hangover from an episode is different because you come out of it gradually, still hearing and seeing things but knowing they are not real.

You have no idea what you did or said during this

episode—and you don't until people tell you about it. You hate that you're usually too drunk or too crazy to know how what you've said or done—that your memories are at the mercy of the eyewitness accounts of your friends. You don't really know which you hate yourself for more—the oblivion you can control or the one you can't. Though you always, of course, feel more shame at being crazy.

You sit cross-legged on the beach, facing the Gulf of Mexico, which is choppy with a red tide that has kept everyone away, except the poor who fish to eat. Along with the glass are bits of shells and sand embedded in the cuts in your feet. You walk down to the water and try to clean out the cuts. The gulf is bathtub warm. You hear voices.

You look around. No one is anywhere near you, yet you are hearing several voices talking just out of range of being able to understand what they're saying. The wind talks. The water talks. You answer in nonsense phrases. This happens near the end of an episode. You try to ignore the voices. You know they are not there. You know they are not real.

But of course they are real. You hear them throughout your life. They are as real as a memory or a love affair. They aren't there. They never have been. But they are real.

LATE FALL 1986: Anne kicks you out of her Amsterdam apartment and you run out of money and have to leave Holland and now you are back in Boston and sleeping on your ex-girlfriend Jane's couch with your Walkman on your chest, chain-smoking and snorting Dilaudid and listening to Joni Mitchell's *Blue*.

No one understands the kind of pain you are in. Your pain and loneliness are undocumented in the history of human pain and loneliness—except, of course, in *your* history of human pain and loneliness from the year before, with Sasha.

The T runs through Jane's building after it crosses the Charles River from Cambridge into Boston. Every fifteen minutes, the whole apartment shakes and dishes and glasses rattle and records sometimes skip, so Jane listens mostly to cassettes.

All day and all night, you lie on the couch with your Walkman on your chest and Joni Mitchell's *Blue* playing as loud as possible. Your eyes are closed. You don't move except to smoke cigarettes or drink beer, both of which you can manage while still on your back. Every once in a while, you sit up and crush some pills on what you later learn is the coffee table Jane inherited from her grandmother. And you will, *honestly*, feel like a piece of shit when you find out that you messed up the finish of this heirloom by crushing the pills with a dead nine-volt battery over and over.

One side of the tape plays to the end and you open up the Walkman and flip the tape and listen to the other side. Your life is over. You will never know love again—that much you are sure of.

You get wasted and smoke and listen to Joni Mitchell because, really, only Joni Mitchell has any idea of the amount of pain you are in.

Only you and Joni Mitchell have ever known this kind of love and only you and Joni Mitchell have ever known what it's like to lose this kind of love.

Well, and Bob Dylan. You and Joni Mitchell and Bob Dylan. But no one else.

2012: You've always had an uncanny ability to memorize things. In high school you were part of a study on eidetic memory, and it turned out you unconsciously use a series of random mnemonic devices. For years you remembered more things than you ever wanted to—some worthwhile, some not. You could remember full pages of *The Great Gatsby* or meaningless basketball statistics from your childhood, such as the scoring average, total rebounds, and total assists of every member of the New York Knicks 1973 champion-ship team. Now, when you forget *anything*, it's colored by your CTE fears. You think it's all starting and that someday you will need a note you carry on a city bus, telling people your name and where you live, because you won't know. Forget the name of a writer, forget something you heard on NPR and wanted to tell a friend—forget anything and you are scared shitless.

In May, you try to use your credit card at the gas station and when it asks you for your zip code, you can't remember it. You've lived here for five years. You call your wife and ask her what it is. She tells you.

You're shaking. "There's no way I'd have forgotten this before."

She knows you're afraid. She doesn't like to talk about your memory going. You've made her promise to help you commit suicide before you lose who you are. She says calmly that you're being ridiculous. That, statistically, the odds favor you never losing your mind—at least not early.

She tells you that you could have forgotten small things like this ten years ago and never noticed.

She is right. But what you used to think were the smallest things, you are afraid may now be pieces of the biggest things.

SUMMER 1988: You are at a party at a bandmate's Boston apartment, and you've taken a couple of hits of acid in the afternoon because your girlfriend Jane is supposed to be out of town visiting her folks for the weekend, and you reason that if you are really fucked up you will be less inclined to cheat on her. This is what, in your early twenties, passes for foresight, nobility, and all-around stand-up-guy-ness.

Later, a cold plastic cup of beer sweats in your hand. You sit on your friend's bed, watching his fish as it swims back and forth only on the left wall of its enormous aquarium. The story goes, though you have no idea if it's true, that your friend dropped a hit of liquid acid in the tank once and the fish freaked out for days—swimming at three and four times its normal speed—and now has settled into an aquatic psychosis where it would never venture to the right side of the tank where the drug had been dropped. As far as the fish seems to be concerned, the right side of the tank is where *very bad shit* once happened, and there isn't anything that is going to get him to go back there. If this is true, that fish, that brainless cartilage-knuckle full of prehistoric DNA flip-flopping a slow glide on the left side of the tank is, in its way, smarter than you, who returns and returns and returns and keeps returning in various ways to places where the very bad shit will happen for the next twenty years of your life.

You sit drunk and tripping, thinking about that little fish, and Jane suddenly walks into your friend's bedroom. Because of the party noise swelling and receding with the opening and the closing of the bedroom door, you don't even notice her walking in.

She is screaming your name.

It's the first time you've heard her, but she's saying it with the intensity and annoyance of someone who has had to repeat herself several times.

She grabs your head and forces you to look up at her and screams your name again.

Her beautiful face is full-mooned into your line of vision so that all you can see are these probing eyes attached to the person you love.

"Hey," you say.

"What's wrong with you?" she says.

A valid question, to be sure. But one you are not really capable of taking on right now.

"I thought you were in Rhode Island?" you say, stunned.

"What the fuck is wrong with your eyes?" she says.

"I think my eyes are okay," you say, then start to get scared. You feel for your eyes, half expecting them to be gone or bloodied and dangling, but they feel normal. You blink fast a few times. "What's wrong with my eyes?"

"You are so fucked up," she says.

You point to the aquarium. "That fish can only swim on one side of the tank."

"What the fuck are you talking about?"

"I've been studying it."

She shakes her head. There is no way you can articulate it or explain your desperate desire to not let her down or hurt her again. You want to say, "Don't leave." Or, "I'm surprised and happy to see you." Or, even, of course, "I love you." But you can't. She is beautiful, smart, funny, and talented. She is, in short, everything you think you are not and will go on thinking you're not for more than twenty years. The only thing you can find wrong with Jane is her taste in boyfriends—that she loves you is a blot on her otherwise spotless record, but you are soon to fix that.

There are few worse feelings than watching someone you love, who loves you deeply, come to the realization that they can no longer love you, out of fear for their own survival. This is a lesson, like many others, you will have to learn a couple of dozen times before it sinks into your thick, drug-damaged brain, and you finally grasp that it is not at all cool or romantic to be the drowning man who makes others, repeatedly, decide to go down with him, or leave him to whatever the world might have for him.

"I can't even talk to you anymore," she says.

You reach out to her. "You can talk to me."

She shakes her head, eyes alive with tears as she looks above you at a point on the ceiling.

"You are always so fucked up," she says.

You put your head down. The acid has you in a grip that's making it a struggle to form words. You look back up at her. Her head sways above you.

She says it again, "You are always so fucked up."

"I can't really talk about this right now," you finally manage to say. "I'm really fucked up."

She looks up at the ceiling again and you see a tear drop from her right cheek and fall onto your thigh where it darkens your jeans for a second. She takes the beer from your lap and throws it against your friend's wall and runs out of the room. You sit for a moment, trying to think, losing the thoughts as soon as they come, unable to focus. Where her tear fell has already started to fade and blend in with the fabric of your jeans.

FALL–WINTER 1986–1987: You have started to try and make yourself useful and are cooking every night for your ex-girlfriend Jane. You are still getting over how badly things ended with Anne in Holland. You get a job waiting tables and get to bring home extra pasta and raw vegetables and you start eating better than you have in more than a year. Jane lived in Italy and you make every one of her favorite northern Italian meals that you know and when you've cooked through them all you ask the chef at work to teach you more. For a month, you don't repeat a meal. Some nights, you fall asleep in her bed, but you haven't had sex again yet.

One night, holding you, she says, "I'm sorry that this Anne hurt you."

"I didn't do her any favors," you say.

"Still. If you want me to hate her, I will. I get sick seeing you hurt."

You don't say anything.

You start playing your guitar again—the only one that isn't in storage at a friend's rehearsal studio in Cambridge. Jane plays hers. You write a couple of songs together and you suggest starting a band (even though she's already in one), and she looks down and says, "I couldn't be in a band with you."

"Why not?"

She smiles. "For one thing, what am I supposed to do when you're off fucking the bartenders?"

Once. Bartender. Singular. But, still, she has the high ground on this one and while you might be accurate in correcting her, you would still be wrong.

You tell her you are falling in love with her and she frowns with what looks like a combination of hurt and anger. She says, "Don't ever say that to me again unless you are going to keep saying it."

You did let her down very badly once. You vow not to say you love her again until, and if, she says it.

You have always had trouble sleeping. And when you do sleep, you have alarmed many of your lovers, because you often wake up shaking and out of control, in panic attacks that sometimes come in waves, one after the other. Though they usually last only twenty or thirty minutes, it's an hour or two before you can get back to sleep. You have trouble breathing—you can never draw a deep breath. It doesn't matter if it's thirty or ninety degrees out, you always wake up freezing.

You wake up one night on Jane's couch having an attack,

shaking and afraid and you at first don't realize it, but she is cradling your face in both hands and looking into your eyes with more tenderness and love than anyone has ever shown you.

She says, "I'm so sorry, sweets," and she kisses your eyelids and slides under the coat you use as a blanket on her couch and falls asleep with you. Sometime in the middle of the night, you wake up again and she calms you down and takes you to her bed.

In the morning, even though it's still winter in Boston, the light comes through the bedroom window and heats up her little shitbox of an apartment so much that you don't need blankets on her bed.

She puts on this experimental music she's been working on. A friend of hers does heart studies at Mass General, which is across the street, more or less. The friend tapes patients' hearts on ninety-minute cassettes and gives them to Jane to tape over for her band demos. But she has kept some of them with the heartbeats going *whoosh, whoosh, whoosh* for ninety minutes, while she plays textured experimental beautiful guitar and piano underneath the sound of the hearts. Her friend has told her many of these are from the hospital archives that go back twenty or thirty years, which means many of the heartbeats you're hearing belong to dead people.

"This," Jane says, "is the last of their hearts. Ever."

You start to go down on her. You lick and kiss her lips and her clit and her thighs and at times her feet and toes and back to her clit and lips. You suck her labia in time with the hearts and try to do it so gently that you can feel her pulse. It's when you have gently rested your lips on her clit that you feel the pulse of blood through her body and you hear her breathing and you realize she is in synch with the hearts on the tape. The tapes are ninety minutes, but they flip and repeat when one side is done and you want to make this last as long as possible because it's among the most *connected* experiences you've ever had with another person.

The sound of the hearts and the music on the tape gets muffled beautifully now and then when she closes her thighs over your ears. You will always remember her legs. Once, she roller-skated into an ice-cream place where you were the manager. She wore shorts. Her thighs were muscular and tan and you wanted to trace every minor striation and every vein on her leg with your lips.

This rhythm is beautiful, feeling Jane's body so in time with everything in the room. You have two fingers each in her ass and pussy—your left hand angled uncomfortably above your right—and you keep them going in and out in time with the heart on the tape and the pulse of her body. You feel your fingers rolling over each other through the skin, going different directions over and over, slowly— only speeding up when Jane's pulse speeds up and goes off rhythm from the hearts on the tape.

The T runs every fifteen minutes and rocks the apartment over and over. You lose track of it, lose track of how many times the tape clicks over and you only know that a lot of time has passed because the sun left the window and then, slowly, the bedroom got darker and darker and now it's evening.

Afterward, you hold each other for more than an hour. One of you and then the other says "We should get something to eat" so often without either of you moving that it eventually becomes a joke.

With the apartment totally dark, Jane lights two candles—one on each night table on either side of the bed. You both get under the covers and she rests on your chest and every fifteen minutes, the T shakes the apartment. Plates and glasses rattle in the kitchen. The candle shadows flicker and flutter more against the wall when the vibration of the train builds and then peaks, and then everything settles down again until the next one goes by.

9

1990: You drive twenty-three hours straight from Amherst
on speed to visit Mary in Florida. Since Humboldt, you have
been very careful to never drive drunk, since you know
you will not always be lucky, so you have a serious case
of the shakes when you finally arrive. Things between you
seem fine until the second night. Actually, things between
the two of *you* still seem fine the second night. The problem is this guy Jimmy who's over at her apartment hanging
out with you and her roommates. He seems annoyed with
you before you've said five words. Everyone is drinking.
Her roommates go out to hit some bars and you figure this
Jimmy guy will go with them, but he doesn't. You wonder
what his deal is.

You end up playing Mary a tape you and your friend
Rick recorded in his basement of the two of you working
up new songs for the band, plus a couple of Neil Young

covers from *On the Beach* and a drunken version of the *Gilligan's Island* theme sung to the tune of "Stairway to Heaven," which you don't even remember doing, let alone recording. Mary knows Rick. You're pretty sure Mary has even slept with Rick. He's part of a group who all went to high school together, the sort of group where, by now, every woman has fucked every man at least once.

When the *Gilligan's Island* theme is over, Jimmy says, "Where the fuck do you get off making fun of Zeppelin?"

You have no idea what to say to that.

"We were drunk," you say. "Just goofing off."

He looks like he wants to kick your ass. He's a shrimp, maybe five five, but he wears a flannel shirt with its sleeves cut off at the shoulders and totally unbuttoned and he's cut and wiry and he has abs like Bruce Lee and he carries himself like a man who not only likes violence but like someone who seeks it out. You've had your ass kicked. It doesn't hurt the way people think. You're not afraid of him. But you still want no part of his shit and you just want Mary to get rid of him.

Mary senses the tension and, after a while, she tells you she's going to walk Jimmy down to his truck. You're relieved the guy is finally leaving and you'll get to be alone with Mary.

It's just you in the apartment for about ten minutes so you start to feel awkward and wonder where she is. You grab another beer and go out to the third-floor patio and see that Mary's still talking to Jimmy by his pickup truck. It feels wrong to be watching them, like you're interrupting, or spying, so you go back inside and lie on the couch and chain-smoke and drink two more beers.

You go out to the patio again and now his truck is still there, but you can only see Jimmy sitting in the driver's seat. At first you figure Mary's on her way up, but then it seems like Jimmy is talking to someone. Plus, he's not leaving. You can't see the passenger seat, but she has to be sitting there. You wonder what the hell's going on.

You piss and grab another beer and by the time you check from the patio again, the truck is gone. And, you realize a few minutes later, so is Mary.

You sit drinking beer on her patio as bugs the size of small birds pile-drive themselves into the porch light. You turn it off and brood in the dark. You think, of course, that she may be fucking this guy. But maybe it's not about you. Maybe Jimmy is having some kind of problem and she's just talking to him. But that doesn't really explain leaving.

More than an hour passes. You are too drunk to walk straight, but you are out of beer and you decide to go and find a liquor store.

As you get ready to leave, it never even occurs to you that you don't have keys to this apartment. Or that Mary or her roommates might not be home when you get back. It only occurs to you when the door clicks behind you.

You scream "Fuck!" And then realize that drunk men screaming fuck just outside the lobby without keys are men who spend the night in a drunk tank. You walk off, smoking, trying to remember which direction the liquor store was. You wander the unfamiliar streets of Sarasota for about half an hour before you find one.

You only have enough cash on you for a six-pack of Mickey's Big Mouth and two airplane gins. You don't need smokes because you always buy a carton when you hit Virginia, a tobacco state where they barely tax the things and pretty much give them away. You think it's how they get people to move to Virginia. People like you, anyway.

You don't risk drinking the beers on the walk back, but you kill both dinky gins. When you get back, no one is answering the buzzer. The porch light is still off. You think about buzzing a neighbor, but then you'd be no better off. You'd be in the hallway, still drunk and still conspicuous.

You're pissed and thinking, *What the fuck did I just drive here for?*

You wander off to the darkest corner of the parking lot and start drinking your beers. You sit smoking and ducking out of sight whenever you see a porch light come on or car headlights sweep by. Whenever you hear a car, though, you wait and watch for lights to come on in Mary's apartment.

You're almost drunk enough to pass out when you see a guy come out onto his patio and look your way. He walks back in quickly. Right away, any trouble with Mary is forgotten and you start convincing yourself that he's calling the cops. You leave the beer and walk out of the apartment complex. If the cops have been called, you don't want to be on this street, so you end up walking all over Sarasota as steadily as you can. You piss behind darkened trees. It's after two and the bars are closed. You think her roommates must be back by now, but you're afraid the cops are waiting for you.

It takes another hour before you feel safe heading back

to Mary's. The roommates, if they're home, are asleep. The lights are off.

You are starting to get sober enough to explain yourself, so you stay in the parking lot, sitting on the curb and smoking. You walk over to where you left your beers, but they are gone. You go back and smoke on the curb. Cigarette butts are crisscrossed at your feet. Your throat is raw. You wish the liquor store was still open.

Not long before dawn, Jimmy's truck pulls into the lot. You sit there, staring. You're not going over and you hate yourself because, while you are mad at Mary, you are much more relieved that you are no longer alone. You feel pathetic. Someone with a spine would tell her to fuck off. You just want to thank her for coming back while it still feels like it's night and not the next morning.

Mary sees you from the truck. If they were going to kiss goodbye and give you some hint as to what is going on, they won't now.

She gets out of his truck and he pulls away, having the balls to give you a dirty look before he turns around. Mary's walking unsteadily, looking a little drunk, toward you and you try to see if her clothes look the same as when she left, of if they look like they've been off and then back on. Her head is shaved, so there's no way to judge from her hair. She's in low-waisted jeans and a tank top. The same necklace and series of metal and black rubber string bracelets. You forget everything for a moment and just look at her and think how beautiful she is.

Your happiness and relief at seeing her again outweighs

your anger, and you hate yourself for this. You *should* be mad. You should scream your fucking head off.

She says, "What are you doing out here?"

You snap. You do yell. "Where the fuck have you been?"

"Jimmy needed to talk."

"Jimmy needed to talk? *Jimmy* needed to talk? Who the fuck is Jimmy? Did he just drive halfway across the country to see you?"

"He's a friend."

"A friend?"

"He's a *friend*." She has her keys out and is walking toward the door. "And keep your fucking voice down."

"Why the fuck couldn't you just tell me you were going somewhere?"

"Will you please keep your voice down?"

You are in the lobby. Some guy is pushing an industrial vacuum cleaner and you don't say another word until the two of you are alone in the elevator.

You think about screaming, but you end up sounding weak and pathetic. "You just left me."

She's staring straight ahead. "You're drunk. *I'm* drunk. Can we talk about this in the morning?" She closes her eyes and rubs her temples. "I'm fucking exhausted."

"*You're* exhausted?"

"Enough!" she says. Then, quietly, "Please." She looks in your eyes. You will never know exactly how to read this look. She seems exasperated with you, but she looks at you with as much love as you have ever seen. Whatever you could say couldn't mean as much as those eyes.

She says, "Can we please, *please* just end this day?"

You have no idea if she fucked Jimmy or if he just needed to talk and she got roped into something she hadn't planned on. You could ask her if she fucked Jimmy. Later, when you move to Sarasota to live with Mary, you and Jimmy will actually become good friends. You will have a lifetime of opportunities to ask either of them about this night, but you never will. You and Mary are still close. You could text her right now and ask if she fucked Jimmy that night. The answer wouldn't matter now. It wouldn't have mattered much then, really, you realize. It wouldn't have changed a thing. As long as she came back.

You tell her, yes. Yes, of course. Of course, we can end this day.

2013: Whenever you are at all short or rude to Gayle, you end up thinking she will know the real you and leave you. You apologize profusely when you have done something wrong. You also apologize profusely when you've done nothing wrong. You apologize to friends for calling them or e-mailing them. You feel like you're an intrusion in almost everyone's life. Sometimes you walk into a room and the first thing you say is "I'm sorry."

LATE SUMMER 1988: Jane has kicked you out of her apartment and you sleep at your friend Jay's rehearsal space. Jay used to be in a band with Jane. She fired him. He jokes that you've both been fired by Jane.

The building's an old factory warehouse and Jay has

turned the enormous second floor into six rehearsal rooms and one main recording room. There are couches all over the open spaces, but no beds anywhere. Technically, no one is allowed to live in the building—it's zoned commercial—but Jay lives there along with his artist neighbors, who crash upstairs. The only working bathroom is the one that must have been the men's restroom when it was still a factory. The women's bathroom has a giant sheet of plywood screwed over the door and a hideous smell that forces you to hold your breath while you piss in the men's room next door. There are three urinals—only one functional—and a stall with no door. You've been in drunk tanks with cleaner toilets. There is no shower. You bathe, when you do, in a deep sink that also serves for doing your laundry and dishes. Though there aren't a lot of dishes—you and Jay buy takeout when there's enough money left after drugs.

When you first get here, you sleep on one of the couches that faces a window with a view of Boston—the lights of the South Side swelling into the affluent glow of the Back Bay and then the financial district. The city blinking with life and promise. You can't see Jane's apartment from where you are, but you know exactly where it is and you know you could point to it if not for the tall buildings in the way and you look out the window at night with the beauty of the city shimmering and you wonder how you fucked up again and you wonder how many more years you can live the way you do.

Still, the great night view cheers you at first, but then you realize that bands are booked for practice at all hours.

The lights are on and the noise is deafening in the main room, so you move to the floor in an equipment-storage room leaving that view of the buildings between you and Jane. It's not comfortable, but it's the only room Jay never rents to bands, so no one will come in and tell you to move so they can make some god-awful racket they think someone might actually pay to listen to.

You haven't played guitar in weeks. You left one at Jane's apartment—not your best but still yours—and you don't know if you can or will get it back. You start to wonder if you will ever care enough to be in another band. You care less about making music every day. Your bands keep falling apart and you don't have the energy to start another. You audition for one, but by the second practice you realize you are way too much of a control freak to join anyone else's band.

You think that maybe it's time to do something other than music, but you have no idea what. Jay gives you keys to the studio. The building is within a block of a liquor store and a Chinese restaurant that has greasy steam tables where every dish is a dollar.

You lock yourself in the storage room and you turn out the lights and you drink and take ten or fifteen Valium a day and fade in and out of sleep while you listen to Richard and Linda Thompson's *Shoot Out the Lights* over and over. You listen to it so loud that you don't hear any of the bands that are practicing, though you feel the vibrations from the bass and drums in the floor and walls. *Shoot Out the Lights* is a whole album that's centered around the breakup of a relationship—sung by a couple that was breaking up while they recorded it. It's the perfect soundtrack for what you're going through.

You listen to it as closely as you can and you're drinking and you think of Jane and after a while you realize that the whole record has this brilliant musical parallel to its emotional content. The songs are about love ending, about the lingering pain and love left when it's over, about the nature of unresolved emotions. And after listening to the record nonstop for days, you realize than none of the songs resolve musically. The songs don't end on the root note— which would make them resolve pleasantly to the ear. They end on unexpected unresolved chords—the fourth or the fifth. Form perfectly meeting content. You think Richard Thompson's a genius for making an album whose lyrical content is about the unease of a lack of emotional resolve and then writing music that mirrors that discomfort. You think *you* are a genius for recognizing what Richard Thompson must have only put there for very smart, incredibly perceptive listeners.

You listen to *Shoot Out the Lights* and you read John Cage's essays on melody and dissonance. About how any dissonance that resolves to melody is ultimately pleasing to the average human ear. And how any melody—no matter how beautiful—that resolves to dissonance actually hurts and disturbs the listener.

How things end, in music—how they resolve—that's what defines the whole experience.

At night, you lie in the dark and listen to *Shoot Out the*

Lights and you think that no one except you and Richard Thompson could possibly understand the agony of love gone to dissonance. No one could know how this lingering pain could feel, except for you and Richard Thompson. And Joni Mitchell. And Bob Dylan.

2011: The eastern cougar, native to eastern Canada and New England, is declared extinct.

2003: You are about to play your first sober show. Ever. You played your first show in 1979 when you were thirteen years old. You are thirty-seven years old. You have been onstage for years, but never like this. Never this raw. You are ten years clean and you are shaking—not just your hands but your whole body. Every molecule of you vibrating at once the way it does when the train comes into Union Station. You have no idea what to do. You want a drink. You would rather be loaded and alone than clean and with people. And you are scared shitless.

1986: You are in love with Lisa, who once left you for a woman but is now sleeping with you again, and she has always wanted to fuck on a bed of rose petals. She has had this fantasy for years. The night before her birthday, you and your friend Nick pull every last rose from the Boston Common. You pay Nick with a baggie of pot and he wanders off down Charles Street. You put the clipped rose heads in five-gallon paint buckets and carry the buckets over to Lisa's apartment and you pluck all the petals and spread them on her bed before she gets home from her late poetry class.

It does not end well. Roses have insects. Lots of them.

But at least you tried. And you showed Lisa that she most certainly did not, from then on, want a bed of rose petals.

1987: A guy you play guitar with named Mick tells you, "You seem to fuck a lot of lesbians."

1990: Your dad's father is dying. His last words to you are: "If you are going to try to fuck every beautiful woman in the world, you are going to die an unhappy man. And take care of your feet."

Over the years, you will find he was right.

2013: Suicide is the tenth leading cause of death globally.

By 2010, the Golden Gate Bridge has had more than 1,300 people kill themselves by jumping off of it since its opening in 1937.

So many people had killed themselves at the Luminous Veil in Toronto that they built barriers to prevent jumpers. The same measures have been taken at the Eiffel Tower and the Empire State Building. In 2014, plans to install a barrier on the Golden Gate were approved.

These measures are considered to be effective. At least they may be effective at stopping people from killing themselves in those specific places. There's no way to tell if any suicides have been prevented or not.

When you think about killing yourself now, you try to remember, no matter how bad it gets, an interview you read with a man who had jumped off the Golden Gate and somehow managed to survive.

He said that the minute he jumped, as his free fall started, he thought: *I think I just made a terrible mistake.*

You try to remember that. Always.

1985: You are in Amsterdam, at a party with some friends. You're on a semester abroad and classes are held in this bizarre castle maybe fifty kilometers south of the city. But you love Amsterdam, and you spend as much time as you can there. You will eventually go back and live there until you go totally broke and have to leave.

But one night you are playing guitar at a youth hostel with some guy who only knows Talking Heads songs. He sings "Psycho Killer" entirely in French. You just play along and you all drink and smoke hash. Eventually he asks if you'd like some heroin.

You never turn down drugs—even drugs you're not that fond of. But you've never tried heroin. A ton of your heroes have been junkies. You have romantic ideas about it. You think of Miles Davis, of Keith Richards, of Johnny Thunders. It doesn't really occur to you that it pretty much destroyed their lives.

You snort a line. Very soon, you are calmer and happier than you can ever remember feeling. It's a perfect waking dream. It's every beautiful moment, amplified all at once. You love everything around you.

It's like someone pulled a plug at the bottom of your brain and all the tension and insecurity and self-hatred just drained away. It's like you are living in someone else's body. Someone not at all like you. Someone happy.

You ask this guy where you can buy some heroin.

1972: You are at the dinner table with your family. You dread family dinner. You dread the fear that starts about an hour before your father comes home. Two years after this, he will get a job as a narcotics officer with the state and he will become a much nicer, much less stressed and angry person. But he is working eighty hours a week at three jobs as a pharmacist, which he hates. Most nights at dinner, you never see his face. You only see the back of *The Bridgeport Post*. When you annoy him, he folds down a corner of the paper and tells you to please give him a moment's peace. This often gets your parents arguing, adding to the long list of reasons you dread dinner.

You will never remember what else is on the dinner table this night, but the vegetable served up is brussels sprouts. You hate brussels sprouts. The smell alone makes your stomach flip-flop like a fish on a dock.

You try to eat one, but you can't. If the smell is this bad, how can you possibly put one in your mouth and chew it?

"May I please be excused?" you ask. This is what you say in your house when you want to leave the dinner table. It may be the only formal thing about your parents.

"Not until you finish your vegetables," your mother says.

"I can't."

"You *will*," your father says. "This isn't a debate."

You know you can't chew them, so you cut them in half and start swallowing them like big pills washed down with your milk. You get most of them down this way, but then one gets about halfway down and threatens to come up. You barely keep it down.

"I can't eat any more of these," you say.

"I said this isn't a debate."

You are getting desperate and angry. "If I eat another one, I'm going to puke."

Your father says, "You puke and you'll eat it."

You are not thinking—well, you're not even capable of thinking that your father is getting his ass kicked by the world eighty hours a week at a job he hates. You know your parents argue about money all the time and there's a ton of electric stress in the house. But you don't know they've moved to a town they can't afford so you and your sister will be safe and get a good education. You aren't thinking about how he coaches your junior league basketball team or your little league baseball team. You aren't thinking about anything you might like about this man. You are only small and you are filled with rage and hatred and anger and fear. You are shaking and you feel like you might piss your pants. You father stares at you.

You try to force down another half brussels sprout with your milk and you puke. The vomit hits your plate dead center but sprays milk and whatever else you ate for dinner—something that looked like spaghetti sauce—over the sides of your plate onto the circular wooden dinner table.

Your father makes you eat one brussels sprout off your puke-covered plate and you do. You fight to keep it down and feel puke rise into your throat but you stop it. Your mother yells at him. This may be one of the times she threatens to leave him.

You will always remember that taste. That smell. That feeling that you can't wait until you're big enough to kick the shit out of every adult you know. Starting, yes, with your father.

You will feel guilty about this urge for years.

He should not be defined by this one action.

He's a good person.

He sacrificed for his family. He worked on himself for years, to the point that he stopped being the angry man you grow up with. He grew up in a house that would make yours look like *The Brady Bunch*. His parents were terrible and incredibly neglectful and your childhood is better in every way. He will loan—and even give—you thousands of dollars when you need it. You will become much closer over the years, even if you never totally understand each other. He will do the most we can ask of anyone—he will do his best.

You will tell this story for years—about the time your father made you eat your own puke. Some people will think it's horrifying. Some won't believe it. Some will think it's funny—and you wonder what their childhood may have been like.

Over the years, you will come to not trust the story as you tell it. You know for sure it's *not* a lie. But what if you are remembering it wrong? The least reliable thing in a court of law is eyewitness testimony. What if your dad never made you eat your own vomit? Then it should never be here in this book. Sure, it's emotionally true—you are terrorized in this way throughout your childhood. And you are almost positive this happened exactly as you will always remember it.

Even if it's true (and you swear to the best of your ability that it is), is it ethical to reduce your father to this one act when he does so much good over the course of your life? You have never felt guilty telling this story to friends. You feel enormous guilt now.

You ask your sister—you have to make sure—if this happened as you remember it.

She says she remembers your father telling you he was going to make you eat your puke.

"Then," she says, "I ran out of the room. I couldn't watch."

1986: You are living in Holland and you've developed a painkiller habit. You can, most days, get enough drugs to keep you high from a corrupt dentist your girlfriend Charlette knows.

You spend day after day nodding in bed with Charlette, listening to a cassette tape that has the Dream Syndicate's *The Days of Wine and Roses* on one side and the Velvet Underground's eponymous third album on the other side. They may be two of the only perfect albums you've ever heard. They are, without a doubt, two of the most perfect albums to nod in bed to on Dilaudid.

This goes on, you and Charlette alone in your room with this one cassette and your drugs, for maybe a month. When you finally leave your bed, you end up going to a party thrown by some friends of Charlette's at a post-hippie commune.

You black out. You have no idea what happens, but you

wake up in the morning with no memory of the night before. There's a guy from Brazil named Tony standing at the
foot of your bed with an acoustic guitar, singing Springsteen's "Hungry Heart" in a thick Brazilian accent. You
turn to your left and realize you are in bed with Anne—
Charlette's best friend. This is a very bad habit of yours
during these years. You sleep with a lot of your girlfriends'
friends. A lot of your girlfriends' best friends. You have yet
to learn that, even in an "open relationship," fucking the
best friend is not a great move.

Tony from Brazil keeps singing at the foot of the bed.
Anne decides that this is, for some reason unknown to you,
a good time to go down on you. You have a hard time getting into it, with this Brazilian guy singing and looking at
you while your girlfriend's best friend is going down on
your semi-hard cock.

Anne stops for a second. She pukes all over your cock
and then, with a groan, rolls on her side and falls asleep.
Tony keeps playing the Springsteen song. The puke is warm
but starts to grow cool on your shrinking cock and your
thighs. It pools in your navel.

You are nineteen years old. You are starting to realize
you have a taste for some sexual fetishes that many people
think are weird. You are learning about things you enjoy
that six months before you had no idea even existed. You
have just learned, however, that having someone puke on
your cock is not one of your new fetishes.

———

2010: The Urinals play a show where you open for Steve Wynn and the Miracle Three. Steve Wynn led the Dream Syndicate. Twenty-five years ago, in college, you had a poster of the Dream Syndicate on your bedroom wall. Now the two of you are friends. You e-mail each other. He ends up joining your band for a song. You share the stage with Steve Wynn. You may as well be playing with Bob Dylan for all this means to you. It embarrasses you how much this matters, but it does. You think about the three months straight in Holland you fell asleep every night with *The Days of Wine and Roses* playing while you were drunk and high. Steve Wynn is part of the soundtrack of your life.

You are clean. You have a house. You have a job, three books out. You're onstage with Steve Wynn. You think that fifteen years ago, there's no way you would recognize the life you have now. You almost fuck up the simplest of songs thinking about this in amazement when you shouldn't be thinking at all and just playing. You are, for the moment, happy.

1989: You stay with your friend Deb and her numerous roommates, down in the low numbers on Avenue B in New York. There are at least ten people in the apartment at any one time.

One night, you are on an abandoned building's roof and you take acid along with three or four of her friends. You and Deb used to be very close, but something's off on this visit, and her roommates don't seem to like you at all. But, you tell yourself, you *always* think people don't like you and you find out later they do. You tell yourself to lighten up and not worry. Not only do they not dislike you, they probably don't even think about you. You're not the center of the universe. You tell yourself to stop worrying about what other people think because all they are worried about is what *other* people think. You feel more mature just coming to this realization. Maybe you're getting less insecure.

You look out at the city about an hour after the acid comes on full force. You realize that you understand how cities work. You *get it!* You turn to tell Deb that you know how cities function—every single fucking level of how they function—you understand it so well, you may have fucking *invented* cities.

She looks up at you, very confused, and says, "What, dude?"

Her friend looks at you and then back at Deb. Then back at you, and back at Deb. The friend says, "I don't like him."

1985: Of all your head injuries, this is easily the most ridiculous. A gallon can of fudge falls on your head when you're a manager at a Häagen-Dazs. This is one of the rare times you go to a hospital after an injury. Your friend insists—her family has money and she can secretly pay for it.

You have trouble talking that night. This is also the first time a doctor warns you about having too many concussions.

"How many is too many?"

"More than two," he says. "Three at the outside."

"I've had more than that already," you say.

"How many?"

You shrug. The lights in the office hurt your eyes and you want to sleep. "Way more than that." You notice that your words are coming slowly and your tongue feels swollen and you can't totally control it and there are times where you are trying to find a word you want to say and you can't think of it.

He gives you pamphlets you can't read for two days because you're seeing double and any light in your eyes feels like your brain is a throbbing toothache.

He tells you any head injuries from this point forward will only add to what brain damage there already is.

He's making it all sound terribly serious. You're nineteen years old. So you've had a few knocks on the head, so what? "Brain damage?"

"This is a condition of accumulation. You've already *done* damage." He looks at your friend, then back to you. "This isn't some headache. Repeated trauma . . . what you've done to your brain is done. You can only avoid more trauma from now on."

You ask your friend to take you home to bed. The doctor says you can't sleep.

"I just want to sleep," you tell him.

He gets close up into your face and screams, "This is serious! You cannot have any more major head injuries!"

His yelling is like a jackhammer inside your head. He backs away. You're seeing double and fuzzy, and you feel like you might throw up. You say, "It's not like I've *planned* any of these."

1971: The photographer Diane Arbus, famous for her photographs of "freaks" and marginalized people, overdoses on pills and slashes her wrists.

FALL 1986: In Amsterdam, you and Anne have broken up. You've lied to her and said that you'd quit doing Dilaudid and you didn't.

You hang out at a hash bar with your friend Ted, watching Andy Warhol's *Empire*—eight hours and five minutes of continuous footage of the Empire State Building. They show it from midnight to 8:05 a.m. every night in the basement. You buy a ticket for the whole week and you can come and go as you please. Eventually, you will see the whole movie.

The third night at the hash bar—maybe four or five hours in, you and Ted are on the couch, wasted and staring at the grainy black-and-white footage. It's night in New York. Somewhere around the eightieth or so floor, a light goes on in a window at the corner of the building.

Ted says, "What is this fucking shit, man?"

The light stays on for about ten minutes. The window goes dark and only seconds later, the window in the next room to the right comes on. It stays light for another ten minutes. It goes dark. The light comes on quickly in the next window down.

Ted beams. "Dude," he says. "Cleaning woman!"

You will always think of this when you think of narrative. Of the desire to make things that happen have some reason for happening.

———

2012: One day in an MFA workshop you're teaching, one of the students—a quick-witted and sharp, funny woman—asks in front of the class, "Do you have any stories that don't end with you passed out in an elevator, or pissing blood, or in a drunk tank? Don't you have any stories that end with you having a cup of tea and going to bed early?"

1911–1916: Violet Jessop, working for the White Star Line, is on board the *Olympic*, one of the two sister ships to the *Titanic*, when it collides with the HMS *Hawke*. A year later, she is one of the seven hundred and five people to live through the sinking of the *Titanic*. In 1916, while working on the third of the sister ships, the *Britannic*, she survives again when the ship hits a mine in the Aegean Sea. Thirty people die. Jessop survives. She is the only person to be involved in all three accidents.

2007: You still have occasional tremendous pain from the broken neck you suffered in Florida so many years ago. For years, it causes blinding migraines that put you down for days at a time, puking, forcing you to lie in the dark until the pain becomes manageable. They start with auras and a stabbing pain behind your eyes. Soon lights begin strobing and the only thing that helps is to turn the water on as hot as it will go in the shower and steam the room up and lie on the floor in the dark. You have, at times, two or three of these migraines a month, but that pace slows over the years. You still wake up in the morning with terrible neck and back pain. Your surgically repaired right knee feels like there is cut glass under the kneecap. The torn ligaments (five times) in your right ankle make it so that it takes at least fifteen minutes before you can walk without a severe painful limp—before you can walk normally—every morning.

One morning, the pain is agonizing. You ask your wife for one of the pain pills she takes for her condition. You will go over this moment in your head for years after, but it really doesn't seem like that big a deal to you at the time. You have gotten lax in your recovery. You are not going to meetings, and you're acting like being an addict is who you used to be, not who you are. Gayle doesn't know you were a junkie—only a drunk. When you met, back in 1989, she only knew you as a drinker, and even then, you were trying to quit and she only saw you drink for a couple of months before you got together.

You take one eighty-milligram OxyContin and it wakes something up in you. Something horrible. But at first, you don't see it as dangerous—you only enjoy the euphoria and lack of pain. You take some more without telling Gayle. You enjoy playing guitar for the first time in a while. You are better at your job. Things feel great.

1989: You are partying with some friends in Boston. It's around five in the morning and you are so drunk you can barely stand. Your friend Ted mentions the LSATs.

"Gotta take them next week," he says.

"I'm taking the GREs next week," you say.

"I thought those were on the eighth," he says.

"They are."

"Dude," he says. "That's today."

You laugh. "Fuck you."

"I'm serious, dude."

You ask Mary. She laughs and says, yes, it's three hours from now.

You really need to pass out. You wonder if you should just skip it, but you need it to fill out your Humboldt State application.

Around six o'clock, you stop drinking and have a couple of cups of coffee. A friend gives you a one-hitter of blow. At seven thirty, you walk to the Garner Museum, where the test begins at eight.

You will later forget your score. But it's predictably awful. You shrug it off. You've long ago gotten used to disappointing yourself and others. You take some pride in it. Your friends think it's hilarious how much you don't give a shit. If that's where there's a role, that's the role you'll play. You're the fuckup in a group of fuckups. That's just who you are.

2007: You are at your home AA meeting. You are a couple of weeks away from taking your fifteen-year cake.

Everyone there knows an addict can go out at any time, but no one suspects that addict currently is you. You've got lots of time—people ask you for advice. You are using opiates every day at this point, along with large amounts of Valium, but you are careful to avoid them the day before this meeting so that no one can see your pinned pupils and hear your slurred speech. You know they will recognize your symptoms immediately. You are no longer taking your wife's pills—you have a friend who works at a pharmacy in Los Angeles and you are buying more and more from her.

You've become as big a liar as you've ever been. Your lies before didn't necessarily make you a terrible person—they made you a person who was often full of shit—but now you are lying to friends who think you're clean. The people you're lying to are clean themselves and fight a daily battle to stay that way and not ruin their lives. You are letting everyone down, whether they know it yet or not.

At the meeting two weeks before you take your fifteen-year cake, some twenty-year-old kid with six days off meth comes up to you and asks you how to do it.

"I just don't think I'll ever make it," he says.

And you think, *You probably won't, kid.* You tell him, "Just hang in. Just make it through the day. If you can't make it through the day, tell yourself you won't get high for an hour. Or ten minutes. Or five minutes if that's what it takes." You're supposed to give him your number and tell him to call you any time. That's what people in AA do. But you don't.

You go home and get high.

A friend in the program calls you later that day and asks you if you're all right.

"Exhausted," you tell him. "But, yeah. I'm doing okay."

He may or may not believe you.

When you're an addict and people think you're straight, just saying hello is a lie. You stop answering your phone.

You know your friends will take this as a bad sign, but you are starting to not care. Thoughts of killing yourself have already started to crowd your head.

JULY 1991: You are in a drunk tank in Sarasota, Florida. You are praying your friends can get you out tonight. You're among dangerous, violent people. You look around the cell and think that to any random observer, you would win the award for Most Likely to Get His Ass Pummeled. You don't dare sit on a bench. You don't dare fall asleep. You're afraid to piss in front of these guys, but you do have to make it to the exposed toilet to puke at one point. You are in that terrible stage where you are still drunk, but your hangover has already started.

At one point, you do drift off to sleep in the corner on the floor. You get woken up by a lot of noise. All the cops head to one section of the jail. There's no one watching the cell. All the guys in the cell are pressed up against the bars, trying to see what's going on.

The next morning, after the normal drunk-tank peanut butter and jelly sandwich, your friends come and get you and you find out what all the fuss was about. It was the night Paul Reubens, aka Pee-Wee Herman, got arrested for indecent exposure in some porn theater. There must have been ten cops loitering by where he was. It made no sense to even arrest him. It made no sense to have arrested you. You would have gone home and passed out.

You think, *Isn't there any real crime in this town?*

_____

2011: The singer Amy Winehouse dies of alcohol poisoning at age twenty-seven, the age you got sober for the first time.

2013: You look up the date for the night you were in that drunk tank in Sarasota. You could have sworn you were not living in Florida in July 1991. That you were in Connecticut. But you must have been in Florida, since you were arrested on the same night as Paul Reubens, and it's a matter of public record—easy to Google—that he was arrested in July 1991.

Your best guess would have placed that night in 1989 or 1990. You never would have said summer of 1991.

1979: There is a picture of your family at Disneyland. Your uncle and your aunt (your mother's half sister) have taken you to Disneyland because you are staying with them as part of a cross-country trip the summer you are thirteen.

In the picture, you have a three- or four-year-old boy on your shoulders. You don't remember who he was, how he was related to you or anyone else in the photo, but you remember liking the kid. You are smiling—as are your mother and father and sister and an old woman named Hazel who you think is your cousin's grandmother. Everyone seems to be having a good time.

Later that day, when the park is closed and you are in the parking lot walking toward your car, you must say something that pisses your mother off.

She says, "You little son of a bitch," and takes a backhanded swing at your head. You are, at this point, an athlete. Quick. Too quick for her as you duck beneath her swing.

You have no idea when the picture was taken or why anyone was smiling.

You also have no idea what you did to set off your mother, but you figure it is your fault.

You will never forget the look of hatred in your mother's eyes. She later says she's glad that you were too quick to be hit, but you don't care so much about whether she hit you or not. You remember that look.

2013: After only one really bad psychotic episode in nineteen years, you have five in eight weeks in the spring your fourth book comes out.

It really starts the previous July, when you are having fifteen- and twenty- (and one epic seventy-two-) hour manic phases while finishing your new book. You never really sleep very well again after that summer, averaging maybe four or five hours a night, and start cycling in and out of manic episodes and end up depressed enough that you go days forgetting to eat.

On the good side, you lose thirty-plus pounds, and you get your junkie body back without actually having to be a junkie. Your body has only ever looked decent to you if you were using heavily, or when you were doing triathlons for a few years. You only like the way you look when you are treating yourself very well or very poorly.

After seven months without much sleep, things get worse quickly.

After the AWP conference in Boston in early March, you have a thirteen-day stretch where you get two hours max a night, and nothing at all on some. You start having psychotic episodes in clusters.

The first happens on April 1 at the University of Connecticut. You and Gina, who edited your new novel, are doing a gig where you're supposed to give a reading and be guests in a class talking about the writing and editing process. They pay you a decent amount of money to show up and read and not sell books and do your dog and pony show for the students, who seem to enjoy it. You get put up in the hotel on campus. The faculty takes you out to dinner. There are worse ways to spend a couple of nights.

The last night you are on campus, Gina is in your room, watching *Dig*, a documentary about the Brian Jonestown Massacre and the Dandy Warhols. You feel tired and catch yourself falling asleep.

The next—and last—thing you remember is that your legs are restless, very restless. It's worse than the normal leg trouble from your brain stabilizers. This restlessness happens sometimes when you sleep. But it usually happens long after you've *been* asleep and you wake up shaking and sweating. This time all you will remember is that you are kicking your legs and you can't seem to get comfortable.

Gina asks if you are all right and you are embarrassed and angry at yourself and say, "This always fucking happens to me in new places." And then, you are gone.

You will not remember the next several hours. Gina will tell you about them.

Apparently, you are answering interview questions. But no one is interviewing you. Gina is there, listening to you going on answering questions—questions that, if your answers are any indication, are about music. She says the answers are almost coherent—they seem to gesture at context but don't really have any. Later, you are enormously grateful that Gina has seen this kind of episode. That she grew up with a father who had them. That she understands what is happening. Someone else might have called a hospital and you would have been locked up. Few things are worse than that.

Later, you try to go out for a cigarette and she will not let you leave your room. Again, you will not remember this.

You start to come around six or seven hours into the episode. You don't remember anything after your legs being restless, but now you are answering questions that Gina hasn't asked you but you think she has.

She later tells you that she made sure you were all right, relatively speaking, and that she drifted asleep and woke up off and on, while you sat at the desk, talking to yourself and unable to get your headphones working with any consistency. She woke up often to check on you, and you didn't sleep all night long.

It's morning by the time you hear yourself answering what you think is a question she has asked, and this time you catch yourself.

You say, "You didn't say anything to me, did you?"

She's very calm. She tells you, no, she didn't, but that everything's okay.

You walk into the bathroom.

You walk back out and ask, "Why is the coffee table in the bathroom?"

"You put it there," she says. "I didn't want to interfere unless you were doing something dangerous."

You are slowly coming back to yourself. You have lost hours. You have no idea what you may have said. You are horrified at how broken you have shown yourself to be—even to your closest friend.

You apologize, repeatedly.

And she tells you, repeatedly, that there's nothing to apologize for.

Eventually, you must seem to not be a danger to yourself, because she lets you go out for a cigarette. While you brace yourself against the predawn cold in this state where you were born, you start to shake with fear and the realization that this episode could have hit during your reading. At dinner with the faculty. In the Q & A and lecture with the students.

You best friend just saw that you are not always in control of your brain, and that frightens and embarrasses you. The fact is, there is no way this could have been anything but worse. You are horrified that Gina saw you like this. And you are lucky.

1935: The Dutch painter and draftsman Herman Kruyder kills himself in a psychiatric hospital.

2008: You're deep in your opiate relapse and you are stealing your wife's pain pills and you haven't hated yourself this much in years. Just as the lousy person you were came back when you relapsed, so too does your deep self-loathing. What kind of man steals his sick wife's pain pills?

It feels like you have no control over who you are these days. You've tried to quit several times since you relapsed. You still are trying to hide it, but you are falling asleep mid-sentence and always nodding off in front of people. You think you're pulling it off much better than you actually are. You've made it through dopesickness and quit at least four times in the four or five months you've been using. But your shame has kept you from going to meetings, and you can't stay clean no matter how hard you try.

One night, while your wife is teaching an evening class, you look every place you can to find some of her OxyContin, but you can't find any. You look through drawers in the bedroom, inside her vanity and her night table. You're starting to get sick. You're desperate to get high. You can't stand what you're doing, but it's like it has a momentum of its own and you can't stop yourself.

Finally, tearing into her office drawers, you find four OxyContin deep in the back of one of the drawers. At first, you take only two, trying to leave her with some, but you tell yourself she must have some on her and within the hour, you take the other two.

She gets home from work around eleven. You are nodding out at your keyboard. You're supposed to be writing, but you are doing very little of that. You're barely keeping up with a half-assed version of yourself at work. She goes upstairs. You hear her opening a drawer. Then another.

"Fuck," she says.

"What?" you say, though you already know what she's looking for.

"I could have sworn I had some of my pills in my desk."

"Are you sure you didn't take them?" you say. You feel your stomach drop. You've *stolen* medication she *needs*.

Who could look at you and call you a good person? You have a history of being harder on yourself than others are on you. But not this time. This time you're an asshole.

She is frantic. "I was sure I had them."

"Sometimes you take them at night when you're on Ambien," you say. Which is true, in the strictest sense. This statement itself is not a lie. But it's not true in this case.

You say, "Are you sure they were in the desk?"

"I thought they were."

And you help her look. And you think of the saying that a junkie will steal your shoes and then help you look for them. You are a cliché. You are worse than a cliché for your wife. You are someone who hurts her. You are letting her feel terrible pain. What kind of person are you?

EARLY 1971: Your hoarding grandmother, who is taking care of you because you are very sick and both of your parents have to work, makes you eat Vicks VapoRub. Your fever is so high that you are hallucinating that there are worms coming out of the paint on your bedroom wall. A hundred and four degrees at its peak. You are five years old. When your mother leaves for work, your fever is a hundred and two. Looking back, you think that, as a nurse, if she'd known your temperature was going to hit a hundred and four and you were seeing worms, she would have taken you to the hospital.

But your grandmother has enormous faith in the healing powers of Vicks VapoRub, and reasons that if it's so good to breathe in or apply topically, it must be even better if consumed. She makes you swallow three tablespoons of the thick menthol petroleum jelly. The menthol, so close to your nose, makes your eyes tear. Your tongue and throat begin to burn and you can feel it scorch a path to your stomach. Your head still feels like it's on fire from your fever. You *would* still be seeing worms coming out of the walls if you weren't looking at your thighs, doubled over in pain as your stomach burns like those fireball candies you put on your tongue. Only now the fireball is inside you and it feels as big as a soccer ball. You are in agony for another hour. Behind your closed hot eyes, you hallucinate wild colorful patterns that years later you will be reminded of when you see the psychedelic backdrops the Velvet Underground played in front of. Colorful circles are popping behind your eyes for three or four hours. Your grandmother, to her credit, does keep putting ice packs on your head and sits with you. She thinks she is helping, even when she isn't.

By the time your mother is home from work, you are no longer hallucinating and your fever is down to one hundred and two again. Your stomach is killing you and you throw up the Campbell's Chicken & Stars your mother heats for you, tasting hot slimy menthol when it comes up. Your grandmother never mentions what she has done. You have no idea it is wrong, so you don't bring it up either. Your mother never finds out.

This story is another one you will tell for years. Every friend and girlfriend is amazed. Some say you could have died. All of them think your grandmother was crazy. A couple of them don't believe you.

You start to wonder if maybe you're remembering it wrong. She *was* crazy. She filled you and your sister with all kinds of foul-smelling and -tasting things like castor oil, and she would give you a shot of Scotch when you had a mild cold, which you loved. Vicks VapoRub and Scotch were your grandmother's cure-alls.

Your sister is your fact-checker for your childhood. Whenever you wonder if something really happened, you call her and ask. Most times it did. Sometimes you are wrong.

You ask her, "Did Grandma Ament ever make me eat Vicks VapoRub?"

"Twice," she says.

"Not just that one time when I was so sick I was seeing shit?"

"Once when you had the flu," she says. "I was twelve. I told her not to and she slurred some drunk anger at me."

"Twice?" you say.

"If I'd known *how* bad it was for you, I would have tried harder to stop her," your sister says.

"That's like eating a fistful of Vaseline," you say. "That can kill somebody."

You sister sounds defensive. "I didn't know."

"I'm not blaming you," you say. "I'm just amazed I remembered it right."

2013: It's only a month after your total break from reality in the Connecticut hotel room with Gina. You are flying home from the New York leg of your book tour. The tour is going great, but you haven't been sleeping much and in the cab on the way to the airport, you start hearing voices. You are having the start of a psychotic episode at, of all the terrible places this could happen, LaGuardia Airport. There are thousands of people around and you are having auditory and visual hallucinations. You are scared shitless to get on a plane in this condition. You think that you can't take much more of this and you are reminded of Virginia Woolf's last letter to her husband, which began: *"Dearest, I feel certain that I am going mad again . . ."* You wonder if your brain is ever going to fully bounce back this time. Every time you go crazy, it seems to take longer and longer to feel like you can trust your brain again.

People move around you in bovine scrums. You are scared. There are the real voices of the people around you. There is the PA system. And there are voices in your head. And you don't know where one of them begins and another leaves off. It's three hours until your flight. You are afraid to go through security like this. You will be acting crazy. Crazy people are carted away at airport security lines.

You walk out to the curb and light a cigarette and take a benzo and the Abilify you keep only for the start of a full-blown psychotic episode. The good thing about this medication is that it does help stop an episode. The bad part is that it tends to knock you out cold. You take your luggage and guitar and you lie down in the quietest corner you can find. Many hours later, you wake up on a floor in LaGuardia and realize you missed your flight and you are told that you will end up spending another twenty-one hours at the airport before you can get another flight home.

You go on Facebook and ask if any of your New York friends can put you up for the night. Soon, some old friends you would be excited to see under other circumstances volunteer. You tell them you accidentally missed your flight. You don't mention that you are afraid you are losing your mind.

1987: You are home visiting your parents when their phone rings.

You say hello and on the other end, Grandma Ament drunkenly slurs, "You never loved me. No one ever loved me."

You tell your mother that her mom is on the phone.

She sighs and takes the phone from you.

Your grandmother is right. No one in this house seems to love her, though it seems also to be entirely her doing. How someone can live almost eighty years on this planet and have no one who would miss them is a staggering thought to you. All she has left is to live in her house with its pathways through the garbage and to drink and to call her only daughter and tell her that no one has ever loved her.

1991: One morning, while your roommate Brad plays "Strychnine" by the Sonics too loudly—which you would not have thought possible until today—for your ice pick of a hangover, you shit blood for the first time in a while. You are drinking way too much since you went off opiates and are not remembering too many hours of too many days. You've lost track of how many times someone has said something like "We talked about this" when you have no idea what they're talking about.

You mention to Brad that you are twenty-five years old and you wonder aloud how bad it is that you've bled out of every orifice you can think of.

"Really?" he says.

You nod, feeling light-headed and weak. These talks about how fucked up you are have lost a lot of their charm over the years and are starting to be frightening and real.

You say, "Nose, mouth, ears, ass, cock."

He looks at you a moment. He's as much of a mess as you are, so he doesn't lecture. You've admitted to each other that you both plan on being dead before thirty, anyway.

"Not the eyes?" he says.

You think back. Once after a car accident, all the blood vessels in your eyeballs ruptured. You didn't bleed, but the whites of your eyes were as red as a glass of cranberry juice and vodka. You shake your head. "No. Not that I know of."

He waves with his fork. "Then you're fine."

2008: You are six months into an opiate relapse and you're spending many of your days nodding out. You tell people— your bandmates, your colleagues, your students—that you are beyond exhausted. That you've had three jobs, a writing career, and a band that records and tours for years now, and you are simply burned out.

And all of this is true, but it's not the truth.

Your wife has only seen you drinking eighteen or nineteen years ago when you were friends who fucked—when you bounced among six East Coast states in two and a half years and she slept with other friends and couples in California. In the fifteen years you have lived together, she has never to her knowledge seen you strung out on opiates.

You have changed in these fifteen years. People trust you. You don't spend your life apologizing for everything you have done. Well, you *do* tend to apologize—for just about everything, including being in a room—but you don't have nearly as many valid reasons *to* apologize as you used to. People no longer grow sick of you and cut you out of their lives because you have disappointed them too many times.

And now you hate yourself again. You haven't written in nearly a year. You nod off mid-sentence while sitting on your amp at a band practice.

You have to drive to campus for a faculty meeting. You've been dopesick for about twenty-four hours and you know from too much experience that if you can't get anything, you will be in an increasing hell for the next forty-eight hours or more. Already it feels like someone glued sandpaper to the inside of your eyelids. Your shirt is drenched and you're shaking and freezing from the cold sweat. Your car is a stick and your whole body is cramping, but your left leg on the clutch is the worst. Your head aches and you're worried you'll hit the cars in front of you or the cars next to you because you simply cannot focus on anything but your pain.

You think: *I am going to a faculty meeting. I'm supposed to be a responsible person and I am the same fuckup I was.* When the traffic thins, you seriously consider making a hard right into the guardrail, wondering if that would be enough to kill you. And then you shit yourself.

Five years ago, you were teacher of the year and now this.

All this would be fine—well, not exactly *fine* but manageable—if you were not due at this faculty meeting in half an hour. You look at the other drivers—some passing you, and some you are passing. You look at their faces and wonder how great the gap is between who they are and who they know they could be. You're on Interstate 10. The I-10 is known to locals, depending on your direction, as the San Bernardino Freeway or the Santa Monica Freeway. Freeways here, true to the romantic nature of the West and its ever-hopeful revision of the life that came before, are made for movement and the future and they're named for where you're going—not where you've been.

The past, well, that's for when you turn around. Where you've been is only important in the context of where you are. And if where you are this moment is good, the past makes sense and every moment of horror and dread seems worth it. If where you are is terrible, the past just seems like an accumulation of data that confirm you were on this path all along.

How things end up matters.

10

EARLY 2007: You call your hometown police department's hall of records and try to get paperwork on Nicole's murder. You have grown more obsessed with it over the years and have lately been waking up, your blankets kicked off the bed by your restless legs, seeing her bloodied and on the ground, not only in a dream but when you wake up too.

At first the cops are friendly with you. Then you let it slip that you're a writer, and they won't say another word. You are shut out.

2011: Your cousin kills himself by jumping off a bridge in Connecticut. It happens between Christmas and New Year's. You mother calls and tells you about it.

Two days later your parents call to wish you a happy new year.

You father says, "How you doing?"

"Not so great," you say.

He sounds genuinely confused. "Why?"

You pause. "Because my cousin killed himself."

He takes a deep breath and lets it out angrily. It's a sound you know well, one you've hated your whole life, one you catch yourself making when you're short-tempered and pissed off at the world, and you hate yourself when you hear it coming from you.

"Oh, *that*," he says.

And you want to shout, *Yeah. That!* It's been three days. All your father had to say on the subject was, "That was great of him to fuck the holidays for his wife and kids for the rest of their lives."

In his own way, he's right, of course. But it's easy for you to see your cousin's side of things. You only have reports from his brother. That he'd been checked into the psych ward for serious depression and psychotic episodes. That he told his brother the doctors and nurses were spying on him from the mirror and the walls and the electrical lines. He destroyed chairs. When the doctors interviewed him, he was smart enough to say he just missed his kids and he hated being locked up. He wasn't having any break with reality. He was fine.

And they let him go. And he killed himself.

And now a doctor is saying he could have been one of the oldest people on record to have their first schizophrenic symptoms. Through his twenties and thirties he had been diagnosed as severely depressed. But not schizophrenic. Now he's gone. You feel for him. And you are scared for yourself. Not for any late-onset schizophrenia. Just for any bridge that might someday look the same to you as it looked to him.

You say to your father, "Yeah. I'm still pretty messed up by this."

He says, "Let me get your mother."

2013: You publish a novel in which the protagonist's mother commits suicide. You borrow the events and the timing of your cousin's suicide nearly detail for detail. The time of year. The fact that he left his car running on the other side of the traffic, pointed the wrong direction. That it was seven degrees. That the water was well below freezing and he was not found by the search party and would be officially missing until they found him in the spring, like most winter bridge suicides in Connecticut. That there was no note. You use your father's line about the holidays being fucked for the rest of the family. You use every fact you know.

You were selfish to use it in the book—more loyal to the book than to how your family might feel about you using your cousin's death as something so trivial as "material." You wonder about subjectivity and who owns someone's grief and about your own ethics, and you find yourself feeling awful at times about what you've done. But it doesn't stop you from doing it.

2012: You have trouble sleeping. You write Gina e-mails late at night when you can't sleep. Sometimes you aren't really in an episode, but you've been up for days and are no longer lucid, and no matter how much you want to communicate, you can't. Historically, when you're like this, Gayle has taken your phone so you can't send any embarrassing e-mails or texts or make calls you will be horrified by the next day. But now you are often up for days on end, and Gayle's sick and frequently asleep much of the day. You are frequently alone when your swings come on.

You send Gina this e-mail:

"I'm up COUSIN IS aka in the, it's out . WW siciarehbbgg What happen last nigh the point to WHAR GOIN G, just say get Guns. hope your not going crazy with this . . . you seen before golf all asleep at the a report. But at

so much white green)?.58"9!?355? sell in my dory . . . So try hit to push THST hard. I'm skiff arts (kerchief I cease he's ahead of me.

Um sooty it was a main night . . . / -and, I didn't try TI semi it in you I hope you're had jadecsnl"

She immediately responds, urging you to go to bed and not write anyone else.

You remember writing this and trying *very hard* to make sense and get through to her. You believed you had something urgent to say. The e-mail you sent took nearly an hour to write. You couldn't stop yourself. Whatever was in your head seemed enormously important.

You stop trying to get this important message through to Gina. And you don't e-mail anyone else. You listen to her. Explaining this to anyone but your best friend would be humiliating. And she knows this, which is why, no matter how far gone you are, you have trained yourself to listen when she says not to write anymore. You don't always go to bed, because bed can be horrific when you're this wired and awake. But you try very hard to stop sending messages. To stop trying to say whatever it is you so urgently want to say.

1972: You are six years old and you can never fall asleep. You sleep a lot at school and get in trouble, but you are somehow very frightened to sleep in your own room. Once you are put to bed at eight o'clock, you stare at the ceiling. On good nights, you listen to Knicks games on the transistor radio you keep under your pillow. On bad nights, there are no games, so you wait until around midnight, when your parents are asleep, and then you take back to your room every clock in the house that sits on a table or comes off the wall, and you spend from midnight until six taking them apart and putting them back together again.

You know you will be in major trouble if anyone notices a clock or two not working, so you are meticulous. At first, you can take seven clocks apart and put them together by six thirty. A year later you can do it by four o'clock. But that leaves more time to be awake with nothing to do, so you take a couple of them apart again and put them back together.

When your father gets a digital clock for his garage, you try to fix it and you can't. You just put it back together as

best you can and when your father sees it while he's working on a car in the garage, he shakes it. Bangs it a couple
of times. Then says, "Piece of motherfucking shit," and
throws it against the wall, smashing it. You don't mention
that you had anything to do with it.

The digital clocks have gotten too sophisticated for you.
You realize that you can't fix everything.

Instead, you start memorizing basketball and baseball
statistics and counting playing cards. You know Walt Fra-
zier's totals for every year of his career, to the point, rebound, and assist. You know what the last card in any deck
is nine times out of ten. This keeps your brain busy. It's not
as good as drinking your parents' liquor after their parties,
but it helps quiet your mind.

Your dad isn't much for working his brain for fun,
though he is one of the smartest people you will ever know.
He has—before his stroke—a memory that might be even
better than yours, before you spent years fucking yours
up. He could've counted cards too. But your dad also does
stuff, you realize later, to turn off his brain in some ways.
He fixes and rebuilds cars. He tries to teach you, but it
seems too complex and you don't react well to his anger.
The sound of a wrench being thrown on concrete can still
make you jump forty years later.

He tells you it's not complex at all and that you're just not
paying attention. That you do more complicated things all
the time. He says that only three things can ever go wrong
with an engine. Three F's: fuel, fire, and some other F you
forget immediately. He says that once you know everything
that can go wrong, you can fix anything.

You and your father see life differently even then. Before you can articulate it, you know there is no way to tally the enormous number of things that can go wrong, and that too many of them can never be fixed.

But, you suppose now, he knew that, too.

Which is probably why he liked working on engines, where only three things could go wrong and they could always be fixed.

2005: Hunter S. Thompson kills himself with a gunshot to the head. His suicide note reads:

> *No More Games. No More Bombs. No More Walking. No More Fun. No More Swimming. 67. That is 17 years past 50. 17 more than I needed or wanted. Boring. I am always bitchy. No Fun—for anybody. 67. You are getting Greedy. Act your old age. Relax—This won't hurt*

2012: You accidentally take your antidepressants twice in one day. You are on the highest allowable dosage already, and you take your morning dose and then, later in the day you think you forgot to take it, so you take it again. You don't realize what you've done until you are writing an e-mail to Gina and your eyes start to lose their focus. Then, squinting, you try to edit a line in the e-mail. The next thing you realize is that it has taken you ten minutes to write one sentence and your hands are shaking. You tell her this. That your brain feels wrong. She tells you to lie down. You do your best to sign off in a coherent way. It takes another ten minutes to write another sentence.

You lie down on the couch and soon you can't move. And then the hallucinations start. You keep seeing the women you love dying—Gayle, your mother, your sister, your niece, Gina—over and over. You can't stop it. You try to think of something, anything else, but the images of dying women keep coming at you. Gayle is upstairs in her office and you try to call up to her that something's very wrong, but you can't speak. In the rare moments when you are not hallucinating, you try to regain control of your brain, but you can't. You can barely hold on to any single thought, except for one that keeps coming back. You think it's finally happening. That your brain is broken beyond all repair. That maybe you are finally going truly crazy and you will always be like this. You're terrified, and you still can't call out for help. The images keep coming. Violent deaths. Murders, car accidents, drownings. They won't stop.

You end up helpless on the couch for more than an hour before you are finally able to call upstairs to Gayle. She comes down, totally unaware of what's been happening. As best you can, you tell her that you think you took too much of your Wellbutrin and you are not in control of your brain. She asks if you want to go to the hospital and you say you don't know. You're scared to go to a hospital like this. They might keep you there. But maybe you really *need* a hospital. Nothing this frightening has ever happened. It's worse than any episode. You are swollen with dread that it's actually happened: You've gone insane.

Gayle gets online and checks for the symptoms of a Wellbutrin overdose. Some of the first symptoms are hallucinations and loss of consciousness. A third of the people go into seizures. After that, the next two on the list are coma and, finally, death. You're still incredibly shaky, but you can talk again. You're still having hallucinations, but you can control them a little better. You haven't lost consciousness. You tell Gayle that you seem to be getting a little better. That you don't want to go to the hospital. You're worried they might keep you there for at least seventy-two hours.

You tell Gayle you want to lie down in bed, and she helps you upstairs. After a couple more minutes of hallucinations, you ask her to turn on the TV, thinking maybe focusing on something else will help. She flips through the channels while you tell her which ones make your head hurt and which ones feel better. Finally she finds a show that seems to slow down your brain——a show about, of all things, fashion and dressmaking. She stays with you as you stare at the TV, waiting for the symptoms to fade, which, after about thirty minutes or an hour, they do. Now you just feel exhausted and a little paranoid, but you can think again. You are in control of your head.

After a while, you realize you should e-mail Gina and tell her you're all right. You do that, and then you go back upstairs and get in bed. It's about two days before you feel anything resembling normal again.

1984–2013: You have a lot of trouble sleeping through a night unless you're in bed with a woman. Actually, it's only with women who seem to want to take care of you, even if you've just met. You bring this out in women. Everyone you've ever dated has held her hand out at crosswalks to stop you from running into traffic, like you were a seven-year-old. A friend you sleep with jokes that you are addicted to every slutty punk-rock girl with a Florence Nightingale complex.

When you're alone, you wake up frightened and sweaty and breathing hard. You see Nicole bloody and dead. You see your college friend Jim fall off the balcony and die on the pavement three stories below. You see Melissa, raped and killed and left in some alley in Los Angeles. All on a tape loop, over and over. Sometimes, you have anxiety attacks for no apparent reason. The first time you have one, in your twenties, you go to an urgent care clinic, thinking you are dying. You can't breathe and think it is a heart attack. You learn what anxiety attacks are. When they hit, you take as many Valium or Klonopin or lorazepam as you think will put you to sleep but not overdose you. By early 1993, you don't care if you OD and haven't cared for years. By late 1993, you are clean and sober and living with the woman who will become your wife. The panic attacks come more frequently for a couple of years, and then start to slow down to a couple a month. There are eventually stretches of time—a few months, maybe as many as four—where you don't have any and you think they may have ended. They come back and seem to change in frequency for no apparent reason.

1995: After years without any psychotic episodes, a doctor changes your diagnosis from bipolar to chemical depression. The diagnosis, it turns out, is wrong, but you go three years on only antidepressants and you don't have a single episode. You think it's over and you're somehow better, but then they return.

Later, you are rediagnosed as bipolar when you see another psychiatrist and tell him about the manic episodes that accompany your depression. He says he is stunned anyone has ever given you a different diagnosis. "You're textbook," he tells you.

2007: The Urinals are playing a gig at some LA dive and the load-in is in the alley behind the club. It hits you—as it does whenever you are in some Los Angeles alley—that this is where Melissa could have been raped and killed. Probably not, of course. There are more alleys behind dive bars in LA than you can count. But, like it does so many other times, as you grab your amp and guitar out of the trunk, it hits you: This could be the place where it happened.

1988: You are waiting tables at the Marriott in Copley Square. You are a terrible waiter. You can't stand the job and you might be bad enough to get fired, but you are sleeping with the manager, Kendra, which gives you some job security. She is the first woman you ever hear utter the phrase "thread count" when talking about sheets. She is also the first woman you have met who owns $200 underwear. And she tends to pay for your dinners and drinks. Though she thinks you drink too much and mentions it pretty often and it's getting old.

She's six foot three. You are five eight. You need a pair of phone books if you want to fuck her doggie-style. She has a three-inch scar at the base of her spine from surgery a year ago. You think it's beautiful. She hates it.

Kendra is the straightest woman you have ever slept with. She's so normal, she seems like a freak. You are twenty and she is twenty-five and she has, to your horror and dismay, a retirement plan.

"Really?" you say. "You're planning on retiring?"

"I'm not planning *on* retiring," she says. "I'm planning *for* retirement."

You just look at her. She looks like Julie Christie.

"There's a difference," she says. "You might want to think about your future a little more than you do."

"I'm not a big planner," you say and she gives you a pissed-off look.

One day at work, a homeless woman comes in and sits in your section. You know her. You let her sit in your section and she buys a coffee and you look the other way while she goes to the all-you-can-eat lunch buffet. The other servers know her too, and no one gives a shit that she steals food from the buffet. She needs food more than anyone who's ever walked into the restaurant. Besides, they throw away buckets full of food at the end of every lunch.

After she eats a couple of plates of food, she goes to the buffet and grabs maybe ten dinner rolls and puts them in a big canvas bag she carries. One of the security guys sees her. You shake your head, thinking if she would just take

the lunch, they might never know, but even paying custom-
ers aren't allowed to stuff their bags with rolls.

The security guard watches the woman and makes some
call on his radio. Less than a minute later, the head of security and another guard join him at the door. They point to
the woman in your station. The three of them triangulate
and treat the whole thing like some risky military operation.

They close in on the woman and they stand her up and
zip-tie her wrists behind her back. One takes her bag. You
can't believe what you're seeing.

You walk over to the head of security and say, quietly,
"Is this really necessary?"

"What?"

"Can't you just ask her to leave and let it go?"

"What's your job here?"

You say, "What?"

"Is it security?" he says. "I thought you were just a waiter.
I didn't realize you were on my staff."

The other two guards are roughly taking the woman
away. She doesn't say a word and stares straight ahead,
looking like she's numbed on Thorazine.

The guy says, "Just do *your* job, waiter. I'll do mine."

You shake your head.

He says, "You got a problem?"

"Did you really say that?"

"Give me your employee ID."

You say, "No."

"Where's your manager?"

You look at him for a minute and you hate him. You wish
for a second you were the kind of man who solves things

by kicking the shit out of other men, but you are not, and besides, he is. Anything you say is just going to make it worse. You need a smoke and you walk past him, through the kitchen, and out the employee entrance, where all the servers and bartenders take smoke breaks. Your friend Janet, who got you this job, joins you.

You tell her what happened and she joins you in complaining about the security guards.

She says, "Bunch of petty wannabe cops. Jesus."

The security guard comes out the employee door and says to you, "You can't smoke here."

Janet goes back inside.

You say, "What is your problem, dude?"

"You can't smoke here."

It is true that there has been some paperwork posted in the cafeteria saying servers can't smoke by the employee door anymore. But none of the bosses care, and they'd rather have you close to the kitchen when you smoke. "That seems to be a matter of some debate," you say.

"Well, I'm here to tell you there's no fucking debate."

You blow smoke toward him.

Without any noticeable irony, he says, "Do you know who I am?"

For a second you look at him. He's maybe ten years older than you. You think: *This is your life. Getting yelled at by some loser.* You take another drag of your cigarette and toss it in the street. You've had it. You quietly say, "You're an asshole, and I quit."

You walk past him and back into the kitchen and he follows you, screaming that he wants your employee ID.

Kendra runs into the kitchen. She has an urgent look on her face and you figure Janet must have told her about you and the guard.

She says your name. "What is going on?"

"I quit," you say.

"What are you talking about?"

The security guard stands next to you and Kendra. "Give me your employee ID. I'm not asking again."

Kendra says, "*What* is going on?"

"What's going on is he is getting written up and he won't give me his ID."

You turn to him. "Fuck off. I quit. Leave me the fuck alone."

The guard says, "You quit?"

Kendra says, "Give him your ID. It's just a write-up."

"If you quit, I have to escort you off the premises."

Kendra says to the guard, "Let me talk to him."

You just want to leave. You figure you can talk about the details later with Kendra when she's off her shift. "There's nothing to talk about."

You punch out and walk toward the elevators, while Kendra yells at you that she wants to talk to you and the guard follows you.

"You're serious?" you say.

"Anyone who quits has to be escorted off Marriott property. That's the rule."

You have no fight left. If that's what he wants to do, whatever. You go to your locker on the eighth floor. You change out of your uniform while the guard watches you. When you're dressed, you toss your uniform in your locker.

"That goes to uniform cleaners," he says.

You don't even look at him as you walk back to the elevator. He follows you all the way to the employee exit. Kendra is there at the employee door and she says, "Just let me handle this."

You can't stand this place. "Look," you say. "There's nothing to handle."

Kendra says, "Don't you ever *think* about your actions?"

You will later wish you'd said, *Don't you ever think about yours?*

She says, "You are such a fucking child!"

You don't say anything. You walk to the bar across the street and you drink what you made in tip money.

Kendra stops taking your calls.

2013: Oddly, you have never been fired from a job. You have probably had more than fifty jobs. And no one ever fired you. You are kind of amazed at this.

1988: Two of your close friends are getting married. You ask your father what you can get them since you don't have much money. They are poor kids—they haven't registered or anything like that. So you ask your father what would be a decent but cheap gift.

"How old are they?"

"She's nineteen and he's twenty-one," you say.

He shakes his head. "Buy them a matching pair of crowbars to pry their heads out of their asses."

2002: You're teaching a creative writing class and you're on break. One of your best students—one of the best you've ever had—asks you how old you are. He's twenty-three years old. A graduate of Yale. You tell him you're thirty-six. You can see him doing quick math in his head.

He says, "So the first porn you ever saw wasn't online?"

You say, "No—it was under my father's bed, like any normal kid. Or in an abandoned shack in the woods."

A woman in class makes a face. "Gross."

You shrug. "That's where our porn was."

The great student who asked you how old you were joins the army and is killed a year after that. At the time of his death, he had published three of the stories he'd written in your class. Three more, his girlfriend tells you, are in the mail, waiting for word.

1984: You are in your friend Carol's dorm room. The woman in the next dorm room comes in. She's someone other people make fun of, but you think she's pretty ridiculously hot. She's maybe ninety pounds. Siouxsie Sioux black hair going in all directions. She wears garters and torn fishnets and cut T-shirts that show her black bras from the side when she walks—if she's wearing a bra. There are rumors she's a junkie. You have never done heroin at this point. Looking back with a little more experience, you will realize she is loaded as she walks into Carol's open door holding a white phallic vibrator, her pupils like a pinhole camera.

She holds her vibrator up. "It's broken." She seems emotional about it. Like it is a pet she has to consider putting down. She holds it out to you while you are looking at her torn T-shirt and garters and fishnets and her raccoon mascara eyes. "Can you fix this?"

Carol shakes her head and laughs. You go to Siouxsie Sioux's room and you see that it just has a frayed wire that you temporarily fix with half of the sticky part of a Band-Aid, telling her you'll fix it for good tomorrow. You want her.

You give her vibrator back and she thanks you. She pauses. Holds up the vibrator. "I kinda want to be alone now, okay?"

You leave and stand close to her closed door until you hear the vibrator—slow at first, then faster. You want to stay and hear her come, but you go back to your friend's room. More than thirty years later, you will write a novel where a woman asks the protagonist to fix her favorite vibrator and he will get laid after he fixes it.

1987: Jaco Pastorius, often called the world's greatest bass player, is beaten into a coma outside a Florida nightclub.

Most famous for his years in Weather Report, he's known as one of the few "rock stars" of jazz. One of the great performers, he coats the stage in baby powder and does James Brown slides and the moonwalk during solo spots. Early in his career, he becomes the most influential electric jazz player in history. In the late seventies, his abuse of alcohol and cocaine increases, as his behavior gets more and more erratic. By the early eighties, his career is almost over, except for short manic bursts during which he can still approach his former greatness.

Friends, even many he's let down countless times, still

try to help. He is in and out of mental institutions and rehab, but he never stays. Eventually he ends up homeless—living on basketball courts in New York City—blaring a boom box with his old music playing, trying to convince people that's him on the recording.

The beating happens shortly after a trip he made to his home state of Florida. Five days later, his family takes him off life support.

1992: You have quit the UMass Amherst MFA Program for Poets and Writers to transfer to Vermont College's low-residency program for the summer, so that you can move to Florida to be with Mary. Even though the two of you have broken up, your plan is to move down to Florida and get her to take you back somehow. It confuses people when you tell them you left Massachusetts and transferred to Vermont so that you could move to Florida.

During the first residency at Vermont, you find out that all the MFA students stay in the dorms that the undergraduates stay in during the year, so you have a roommate for the first time in more than a year. Your roommate, lucky for you, is a pretty heavy drinker as well. And your best friend in the MFA program is as big an alcoholic as you.

You are off your brain meds. The residency is ten days long. You fuck either two or three women. Strangely, none of them gets mad at you, but then women seem to have given up on you as anything but a drunken slut who might be fun for a night but not for anything more than that. People expect very little of you.

One night, the youngest woman in the program comes to your dorm room, where you and your roommate and best friend are drinking. You all have filled empty beer bottles with cigarette butts. She looks at one of them.

She says, "This is like a SmokEnders meeting. Where they make you look at how disgusting your habits are."

Your roommate Joe says, "Oh, we're far more disgusting than that." And he's right.

You end up drinking all night most nights with an out-of-control drunk on the poetry faculty. In the mornings, you have started coughing up greasy chunks of blood. You are twenty-six years old.

When you are forty-five years old, you will publish a story about those ten days and the greasy blood chunks on a literary website and a woman who knew you back then will write in the comments section: "I remember praying you wouldn't die."

You remember hoping you would.

1985–LATE 1990S: You tell just about anyone you meet that you started at the Berklee School of Music before transferring to Emerson College. Why? Maybe simply because you wanted to go there. You only applied, best you can remember, to Emerson—though your mother swears you were accepted in the music department at the Hartt School in Hartford, Connecticut. You are pretty certain this is not true—but you and your mother have highly divergent versions of the facts of your life. In this case, she may well be right. You could ask your sister, but this one doesn't feel important enough to bother her.

But for years you claim to have attended, however briefly, Berklee School of Music. It's possible you could actually have been accepted, if you had applied. Bart, the other guitar player in your high-school band, got in, and he was only a little better than you. You played with some of the people in his dorm—you could have gone there. But you never went there, so why tell people you did?

Your freshman-year roommate overhears you tell his girlfriend this lie and says, "I have no fucking idea why he tells people that." To this day, you're not sure yourself. You think of the Jeff Tweedy line, *All my lies are always wishes.* Maybe, at times, that's all they are.

1990: You get a letter that you've been accepted into the UMass Amherst MFA Program for Poets and Writers. You had no idea that you even *applied* to the school. You've wanted to be a writer since you stopped being able to function well enough to play in bands—no one needs to rely on a writer to not be so fucked up they can't work that day—but as far as you know, you have never applied to any writing programs. Apparently, though, you did.

You are living in your grandmother's hoarder house, drinking and throwing away fifty years of her despair and drunken neglect. Mary has moved to Florida to go to art school. You wanted to go with her, but she talked about how you'd manage a long-distance relationship before she ever brought up you going with her.

Grad school. Why not?

A few days after the acceptance letter, you get a letter from the UMass Amherst Graduate School that tells you they don't really care that the MFA Program for Poets and Writers accepted you because your application check bounced and you have no GRE scores.

You *did* take the GREs, but you have no idea where that paperwork is. Your score was astoundingly low, something you took a perverse pride in at the time. But you call the Program for Poets and Writers, and they tell you they don't care about the score on the GREs, they just care about the writing sample. No matter how bad your score, if you can find proof you took the GREs, you're in.

1992: Your friend and mentor François, who for the rest of your life you will half jokingly refer to as "Dad," has brought you out to a writer's conference in Utah. He used to be on the board and he tells you he got you a scholarship, but you will learn later that this is not true—he knew you couldn't afford it and paid your tuition. You never would have let him do it if you'd known, which of course is why he lied.

Before you head to Utah, you need a haircut, but you never get around to it, so you just shave your head the morning you fly out. François tells you this is a chance to meet some editors and agents and to get your writing looked at by people who can help your career, especially this editor Amy, who has published François and who edits at a glossy that pays thousands of dollars for a story. He tells you that you need to get her to read your work. He tells you she'll probably get drunk and want to fuck you. That's just what she does at conferences.

The first night, you meet Amy, who's really attractive

in a bossy sort of way. She wears clothes that probably cost more than your car and she always acts like she's the most important person in the room. The second you meet her, you dream about being her secretary and being told what to do by her all day.

The second-to-last night of the conference, Amy sits next to you at dinner, drinking wine and rubbing your shaved head and telling you that you should grow your hair out and saying what a pretty boy you are but that you'd be so much prettier with hair.

"Done," you say. "Whatever you say."

"God," she says loudly to people at the table. "I just met a writer who says *whatever you say* to an editor." She rubs your head again. "You could all take a fucking cue."

You end up fucking in her enormous suite in some Park City condo.

The next morning, after Amy has left the conference, François says, "So things seemed to be going well with Amy."

"Yeah," you say. "She's pretty great."

"Did you give her your work?"

"No."

"What? That's why I *brought* you here."

"It seemed rude," you say. "I mean . . . we were fucking. It seemed pretty tactless to ask her to read my stories."

"That's why she's here. To meet writers. To fuck writers. She fucks young writers and she reads their work. It's what she *does*."

"I'm sorry," you say.

"You need to write her a letter and get her to read your work."

"I'm not sure I can do that." You are thinking, *There's no way I can do that. I can't even call for a pizza without having an anxiety attack. How can I ask an editor to read my work?*

But you do it. You do it because you don't want to let François down and you promise him you will.

You write Amy and ask if she'll look at some of your stories and to your amazement she writes back, "Of course. I'd love to see what you have for me."

You read the letter several times. What you have *for me.* Your stories are for her—she's already decided. You see your name in her glossy magazine. You see others in your future: *Granta. The New Yorker's* "20 Under 40." You're on your way.

Amy writes you back a few weeks later: *These stories show some promise, but they are stiff and wooden and derivative. You should write more like you fuck.*

1985: You find out that heroin is illegal in Holland and comes with a stiff jail sentence. Jail scares the hell out of you. You aren't as risky as some of your friends. You won't buy in a shooting gallery. You won't even shoot it when you have it. You find a less dangerous way to get high, via your girlfriend's dentist. You actually *do* have severe pain under one of your molars and it turns out to be an abscess. The dentist gives you Dilaudid for the pain. Dilaudid turns out to be as good as heroin. But you figure you can't go back to the doctor and get pain meds unless there's some real trouble again. So, you take a rusty screwdriver and you dig at the flesh where the abscess has started to heal. This actually hurts more than the original abscess, but you need the drugs. You can feel your pulse, angry and hot and aching, on the whole right side of your face. You see the dentist and tell him you're in terrible pain, and he looks and asks you what happened, but you play dumb and say that the infection just got worse. He cleans it out and gives you more pills than before.

You do this again when you run out of pills. You cut yourself until your gums bleed. This time, when the dentist sees you, he invites you into his office. He looks at the gouges and cuts under your lower molar.

He says, "You do not have to keep doing this."

"What?"

"You need the pills, I give you the pills."

You are stunned. Free nationalized health care is one thing. Free health care where a doctor will give an addict their drug of choice? It's heaven on earth.

From then on, you pay him for the pills. Not a lot. Cheaper than a dealer would charge. Well, of course, he *is* a dealer. But it's neat. Professional. You sometimes use too much and end up short for what you can afford and go through dopesickness. But, for the most part, you are kept in Dilaudid until you fly back to the States in 1986.

2008: You are playing guitar with your friend Billy. He's a real guitar player, a professional who plays in Jimmie Vaughan's Tilt-A-Whirl Band. He's been on stage with

Buddy Guy. With Billy Gibbons and Jeff Beck and Hubert Sumlin. He played at Eric fucking Clapton's birthday party at some castle in England that only holds events for people who've been knighted. *Sir* Eric Clapton steps aside and calls for Billy to take a solo when they're playing Freddie King's "Hideaway."

You and Billy are in your home studio, playing a shuffle blues. You have your eyes closed. Billy finishes a solo and you start to take yours. You're playing over the simple changes that Billy—a real player, after all—really knows how to groove on. But, you realize, you actually sound pretty great together. Your solo isn't the greatest thing ever played, but you sound good. You open your eyes and look over at your friend. You think: *He's played with Buddy Guy and Billy Gibbons and Jeff Beck and Hubert Sumlin. He played at Eric fucking Clapton's birthday party! Who the fuck are you to be playing with him?*

You make a mistake. Then another. Soon, you are playing like total shit.

You were playing really well until you started to think.

And then it hits you: Pretty much every fuckup in your life was a result of thinking when you shouldn't have been thinking, or not thinking when you should have been.

1987: You want to take some money out of a bank machine, but you don't know if you have enough. You chose the New World Bank in Kenmore Square specifically because the machine gives out money in ten-dollar increments, rather than the standard twenty. You are close to broke, you know that much. You've just paid the rent, late, in cash. Your original plan was to use the cash for weekend bar-and-drug money, but the landlord actually came to the house and you and your roommates all had to pay up. Now you may not have enough money to eat. You're hoping your balance is more than ten dollars and don't feel good about your odds.

You check your balance. The receipt reads $1,011.22. You stare at it, not moving, until the guy behind you asks if you are done with the machine. You take a few steps away and sit on the stairwell to a second-story business. You stare at the paper. One thousand dollars! It can't be possible. You start to go into the bank to close your account, but then you think that they could find out and this could be illegal. And there is *no way* that you will be able to come up with a grand if they want it back. You toss it around in your mind for hours before you call your boss at the ice-cream parlor, Ron. He's a businessman. He used to run an art gallery. He knows shit about the world that you don't.

"Let me call my attorney," he says and it always strikes you as odd that he says "attorney" instead of "lawyer." Calling a lawyer an attorney reminds you of being arrested. Attorney is a cop word. You have the right to an attorney. You briefly wonder if you could be arrested for taking this money. Would it be stealing? Well, it is stealing, but is it *stealing*? You think about being arrested and you shudder, never wanting to go through that again.

Ron calls you at work the next day. "The only thing they can do is ask for it back."

"That's it?" you say.

"Legally, that's it. They ask for it back. If they ever figure it out."

On your lunch break, you walk into a bank and a woman asks if she can help you. You are shaking a bit. You feel it especially in your knees.

"I'd like to close my account," you say.

She punches some keys and the same magical thousand dollars comes up.

You say, "I'm going to do some traveling." You wonder why you're lying to her, why you're inventing this back-story for yourself. Why the fuck would she care what you're doing with your money?

She counts the money out in crisp hundred-dollar bills and you walk out of the bank with a thousand dollars and change thick and beautiful in your left front pocket. Your plan is to buy a pre-CBS Stratocaster from Daddy's Junky Music. It's at just under a grand and you know, you just *know* that these are going to skyrocket in value. It could be worth five grand in a few years. You see this coming. You're an idiot, but you're not stupid.

But instead of buying the Stratocaster, you call Mike Way, known as "the Way" to everyone who buys drugs from him. All the dealers have cocaine in Boston in the mid-eighties. Nobody seems to be able to get their hands on heroin. Not even the Way. But he can get you some Percodan. At first you buy an eight ball and thirty or forty pain pills. Later that night, you and your roommates are partying and you decide to call the Way and get another eight ball. You are sharing the blow, but you are keeping the pills all to yourself.

"You should have gone with the quarter, my man," he says.

"Wasn't thinking ahead." You tell him to bring at least thirty Percodan as well.

He delivers the second eight ball. Usually you have to go to him, but he's made a shitload of money off of you today and he's acting generous. Well, you suppose he is *being* generous, if he's the one walking the streets with the eighth and not you.

He hands it and the pills to you at the door. "Little extra in there. Went a little heavy for you."

You thank him. Like the Way's a good guy. Like he cares about you.

There are maybe twenty people in your apartment. You have four roommates and each of them has invited people—mostly women—over.

You think of something Mary said once: "If a woman is paying for cocaine, she's doing something wrong."

You get far too drunk and the blow keeps you up much longer than you should be up. If you were just drinking, you would have passed out by now. You are talking nonstop to the girlfriend of the lead singer in your band. She's stunning—she looks like a young Marianne Faithfull.

You smoke three packs of cigarettes. You will stay up far too late saying stupid shit to a beautiful woman, this girlfriend of your bandmate who somehow ends up in your bed at five in the morning. After you go down on her, difficult given your cocaine-numbed lips and cigarette-burned tongue, you try to fuck and your cock is useless from the blow and the pills and the gin and the beer.

Around nine o'clock in the morning, you are spooning her from behind and you start to get hard. You think this is a chance to impress one of the most beautiful women who has ever wanted you. To prove your cock isn't *like* that—it was a one-off deal.

She says, "*Now* you're ready?" She shakes her head and gets up. "I got two hours sleep and I feel like shit." She looks down at you, naked. "I shouldn't even be here." She leaves.

The thousand dollars is gone by the end of the week. The Way is out of pills. You start buying in grams, then half grams, then, out of pity, he sells you quarter grams. The lead singer of your band finds out what happened with his girlfriend. The band breaks up.

2013: The guitar you were going to buy with that magical thousand dollars is worth well over forty thousand dollars now. Though this doesn't really bother you. There's no way you would have been able to hold on to it. You probably would have sold it for drugs not long after buying it. You would have fucked up. You know yourself.

11

1974: The confessional poet Anne Sexton kills herself by carbon monoxide poisoning after fighting depression and bipolar illness her entire adult life. She is forty-five.

2009: You read that your depression is to be expected, medically, even though it's worse than it's ever been. The first year people go off opiates, their serotonin and dopamine receptors are fucked and they are prone to severe depression for at least six months after getting clean, sometimes longer. You have a history of depressive episodes as it is. You go a year without a single manic high. You can no longer write. You read your books and wonder who that person was—how he did it. All you are capable of writing are suicide notes. In nine months, you write forty-seven suicide notes. You are smoking again after eleven years off. You figure you've earned it. You're not getting high. Fuck anyone who gives you shit. You don't plan to be here much longer anyway.

1983: In what you later list as your fifth concussion when you see the neurologists, you crack the back of your skull so badly you throw up while on your back, and your friend Steve flips you over and saves you from choking to death on your own puke.

You are at a basement party in high school and you have a two-liter Diet 7UP in one hand and a one-liter bottle of Canadian Club in the other and you are taking deep swigs of one after the other. The last thing you remember before the sound your head makes on the concrete floor—a hard wet crack—is listening to the Dream Syndicate's "That's What You Always Say."

Your friends have no idea what to do with you. They can't wake you up, so they drive you to your house, leave you on the front porch, and ring the doorbell until they hear someone coming. Just another time that you will only find out what happened because someone tells you the next day.

Your sister finds you on the front porch. She tries to revive you. She tries to wake you up and keep your parents out of it, but she can't.

This is the first time you have alcohol poisoning.

Your parents apparently debate taking you to the hospital, but you slowly come around. Or at least you're talking, if not making sense.

At one point you scream, "There is no sanctuary for you here, Ramon!"

You have no idea what this means.

Your father is cradling your head. His hand, when he pulls it away, is greasy with your blood. But it's just from a crack in your skin from the swelling, not a deep gash that will need stitches. Your father knows that you, besides being very drunk, have a concussion, and he won't let you sleep. He stays up with you all night.

AUGUST 22, 2009: You are two days clean and deep in the throes of dopesickness. You have come out to your wife that you have been using. The night you didn't kill yourself, you came home and quietly put her pills back in their bottles while she was out. You have told her you're going to quit. You have no memory of the conversation you have where you tell her you've been stealing her pills. You remember something she once said about how if you ever drank again, she would leave you. But you're so deeply sick at this point, you're not thinking about that. And, if she did decide to leave you, who could blame her? You think you deserve whatever might come your way, no matter how bad.

You don't remember what you said after telling her that you'd been stealing her pills and buying others on the side. You don't tell her about going out to the shack to kill yourself—the one thing she said she would never forgive you for. You just tell her you've been using and that you're two days clean and getting very sick. You're apologizing over and over and she stuns you by holding you and telling you that everything's going to be all right. You think you don't deserve this—her love—anymore. But you are too broken-down and sick to say anything. You let her hold you for a while before telling her that your whole body hurts so much that you need to lie down.

That night, she goes with you to a meeting, where you face the shame of taking a newcomer chip. Everyone applauds while you go up to get it, and your body aches and you wonder if you did the right thing in not killing yourself. You get a new sponsor and he will call you several times over the next few days, checking in. At first, you're too sick to even talk to him. You are in the guest bedroom, puking and shitting yourself and wishing you were dead.

Later, after you clean up, you will ask Gayle to lock up her pills, so that you cannot get to them anymore. You feel like a child. Like someone who has no control over his desires. But you *are* someone who has no control. She starts locking her pills away, and does this for years after.

But meanwhile, your wife has come back from the grocery store with sweets and juice and everything your new sponsor told her might help you get through the first seventy-two hours. When she comes into the guest bedroom to tell you this, you have just fallen asleep for the first time in a day and a half. Your entire body has been a relentless series of red-carpet flashbulb pops of pain. When she wakes you up you say, "I can't believe you woke me up! Jesus! I was finally asleep!"

You are curled in a ball of pain and the woman who loves you—who has stood by you, who has forgiven you what you can never forgive yourself—is crying in your bedroom down the hall. And you are thinking: *You did this.*

1974: You are having your tonsils out. Everyone has told you that this is a piece of cake. You go in, you come out, you get ice cream and don't have to go to school for a week. What could go wrong?

But something goes wrong. Something makes your throat hemorrhage, so that clotted chunks of blood keep showing up on your pillow every time they tell your mother everything is under control.

You end up in the ICU for a week. The first two days, they tell you that you will be going home soon. After two days, they stop saying this and instead say things like "We need to watch the bleeding" to your mother.

The hospital is undergoing some construction, so the ICU is also housing a kid who would be in the burn ward if there was a burn ward. He is two beds away from you. His name is Ishmael. He moans all night long and his pain doesn't even sound quite human to you—more like the noise of some primal animal's suffering. His mother calls him "Ishy" and cries his name quietly all night long. *Ishy, Ishy, Ishy, Ishy, Ishy.*

You do not know it at the time, but you are hearing what a mother sounds like while she watches her child die. You will never forget it. He will be gone in two days.

You fade in and out of consciousness. You feel like you are swallowing crushed glass. You cough up blood. They put you on meds that have you so loopy you think the tall orderly is Wilt Chamberlain. You love the feeling of the drugs. It's like being awake and dreaming at the same time. You think, *Why can't life always be like this?*

Your mother will never leave your side. Every time you

wake up, you will see her, sitting there, staring at you, holding your hand, not turning around as Ishmael's mother cries *Ishy, Ishy, Ishy.*

2009: About a year after you've cleaned up after your relapse, you are still deep in a daily unrelenting depression. You and your wife are driving home from an Adult Children of Alcoholics meeting and she says something, trying to cheer you up, since it's clear you're down about something. About everything.

You don't remember what you say back to her, but you will never forget her response.

She begins crying and pounding both hands on the steering wheel, screaming, "Why can't you EVER just be HAPPY?"

2013: By most estimates, 99.9 percent of all species that have ever lived on earth are now extinct.

1977: The summer Nicole is murdered, your neighbor—a fourteen-year-old girl named Kim Young, from the religious family who moved into the Meyers' old house the year before—sings "You Light Up My Life" every single day, several times a day. You hear it through her open window.

Mr. Meyer is the man who taught you to shoot a gun. He also once, while trying to chop out a stubborn root from his yard with an ax, cleaved open a three-inch-long by one-inch-deep wound just above his ankle. You heard him scream. You don't remember if your father took him to the hospital or not, but you do remember that for years afterward he would wear the torn sock, never again washed and permanently crusted with his dried blood.

"There were fucking threads imbedded in the bone," he says to you at one point. "How fucked up is that?"

Your mother calls him a lunatic. So does your father. Yet he still had your parents' permission, as best you can recall, to teach you to shoot a gun. He and his wife both drank a lot—though not as much as Mr. Kesler next door. You had a crush on Hannah, the Meyers' fifteen-year-old daughter. The day you go to learn to shoot, she comes. It's why you went. She was going to be there.

Now the Meyers have moved. You have no idea where. When you are a child and people move out of your neighborhood, they are just gone.

Not gone like Nicole, but still gone from your life.

And now Kim Young sings from what used to be Hannah Meyer's window all summer long.

MAY 4, 1932: An unidentified woman is found dead with a crushed skull in Stockholm, Sweden. Police note that someone has drunk her blood and the case becomes known as the Vampire Murder Case. It remains unsolved.

MARCH 2011: For years your liver levels have been a problem whenever you go to the doctor, which makes sense. You have treated it like shit. You get tested at your GP and she doesn't like your liver levels and draws more blood and sends it off to a specialist.

The person who does the test makes a mistake and calls you instead of your doctor. She tells you that "His levels have to be watched very closely. Do you know how much he drinks?"

"He?" you say.

"This liver looks like it belongs to someone who's drinking a fifth a day. You need to speak with this patient."

You say, "What do mean 'this patient'? You mean me?"

The woman on the end of the line says, "This isn't Dr. Hart's office?"

You say no. You tell her you're the patient. "And I haven't had a drink in eighteen years." You don't mention the year on pain pills, which of course would also fuck with your liver.

She sounds flustered. "Well . . . these levels. You should talk with your doctor. I'm not supposed to call the patient. I was looking for the doctor."

"Well you got me. So tell me what you were going to tell the doctor."

"I can't," she says.

"Look," you say, "the doctor's going to tell me whatever you tell me. I won't say you told me."

She pauses. Then she tells you that your levels are too high. High enough to indicate your liver isn't functioning properly. That it looks like something called fatty liver disease. "It isn't always, but it can be."

You hang up on her. You immediately freak out. *Disease?* You start to have trouble breathing and you can feel your heart beating and your pulse pounding in your neck and temples. You can't believe you've tried this hard and stayed clean as much as you have only to have this happen. And then the anxiety takes on a momentum of its own. You feel yourself losing control, like the start of an episode. You are afraid you are going to die. That the damage you have done over the years has caught up to you and there's nothing left that can be done. This woman's just told you so.

Before you know what you're doing, you call someone you knew from AA, someone who has gone out and has been using for a couple of months. You ask him if he can get you some heroin or pills.

"Only blow," he says. "Or meth."

You're consumed with self-hatred. You need, even if it's not the drug you want, to be out of the head you're in. You tell him you want an eight ball. Gayle is off teaching and you leave a note that you're staying over in LA after band practice. You end up somewhere around Banning or Beaumont. You stop on the way and do two lines of blow at a rest stop off I-10.

You check into some shitty cheap-looking motel, go out and buy yourself a fifth of gin, and lock yourself in your second-floor room to do more lines, knocking them back with gin that you haven't tasted in almost twenty years. It's warm. It stings a bit, and you are madly in love with it, despite your shame. You do one line after the other, figuring that in this one night you can't fuck your liver more than you've already fucked it, but maybe you can give yourself a heart attack or can OD. You've seen people die of liver disease, the whites of their eyes jaundiced, along with their gray leathery skin. Toxins flooding their brain. You're not letting that happen to you. You hate yourself for what you've done, but it's too late to change it, so you're ending it.

But by six o'clock in the morning, you're not dead. You're just totally fucking wired. You walk outside onto the second-floor walkway. It's still dark and you look at the streetlights flickering in the distance and listen to the blur of early-morning traffic on I-10 and you chew your gums and you are drunk for the first time in ages and everything beneath you looks small, like the houses and cars and trees of a miniature train set.

For a short time, you start to feel like this would be a romantic place to die. Just end it here in the latest in a string of seedy hotels you've done drugs in over the years. This isn't like your planned overdose in 2009. That was because you couldn't stand to live another fucking day. This is because you can't stand dying on someone else's terms. You wouldn't be the first loser to die in some shithole of a motel.

Even as you are doing the blow and drinking, you know you are making a terrible mistake. You're running low on the coke and gin. And somehow, you start calling yourself on your own bullshit. Depression consumes you as you sit in the motel. If you are going to die from what you did to your liver, well, you are going to die, but not like this. You lie on the bed, call for a late checkout, and stay there trying to sober up as much as possible. Coming up on noon, you realize you are still nowhere close to sober and you check into the room for another day and tell Gayle you're staying in the city with a friend. You try to sleep but, predictably, can't. You think about drinking more, but you don't. You find yourself shaking from the fact that this all happened without any real thought. Like getting loaded was an instinct. Like hurting yourself is, no matter how hard you have tried to retrain yourself, your default setting and you will never, ever be able to change that.

The next day, your doctor calls and tells you that your liver levels are at the high range of safe, but if you take care of yourself, you could live another forty years. The tech at the lab made some kind of error. You feel like an even bigger idiot than you did the day before, lying in that shitty motel room surrounded by empty bottles.

You try to put this out of your mind. You decide that you will not tell Gayle, not tell any of your other friends in recovery. You fucked up. You know it. It's over. Whether you are lying to yourself or not, you will call this a slip and not a full-blown relapse. You will go back and forth on calling it a suicide attempt. Trying to kill yourself is not a relapse, you decide. You have no idea if you are lying to yourself. Some days you think you are, some not. You will not change your sober date.

You tell yourself, over and over and over, that you thought you were better than this.

But you are not.

And you may never be better than this.

APRIL 2013: After attempting to hide your mental illness from most of the people in your life since your late teens, in the end you fall apart in a very public forum.

It's the weekend of the release party for your fourth

book. It's also the *Los Angeles Times* Festival of Books, at which both you and the head of your department, Tod, who is also one of your closest friends, are longstanding regulars, cracking each other up on panels annually. Writer friends come in from all over the country, to what used to be your hometown but now of course you have to drive two hours in from the desert to get to LA. You are still in bad shape, recovering from your psychotic episode in Connecticut a couple weeks prior, still not sleeping more than a couple of hours a night. You feel like hell, although you're consoling yourself that you *look* pretty good, having dropped thirty-five pounds in half a year.

Since you've lived in the desert, you cancel on friends more than you used to—you used to pride yourself on never canceling plans, but you can't be that guy anymore. The truth is that if this were anyone else's release party, you wouldn't be there. But you can't get out of your own party. Your band is playing. Gina's flown in from Chicago in the middle of some crazy Midwestern storm where holes are opening in the street. Gayle has rallied even though she's in pain, has put on a sexy black dress and is driving to LA with you, the first literary party she's attended in ages, excited about plans you've been making to move back closer to the city soon. This is supposed to be your big night. Backing out isn't an option.

Nearly without exception, people start asking you if you're okay from the moment you get to the party. You keep saying you're fine. You *feel* okay once you're there, actually, high on the adrenaline. Your body and brain may have been headed for this breakdown for months, but it's started to feel normal to you. You admit to close friends that you're exhausted, that you haven't been sleeping. This is the truth, but not the whole truth. You don't tell anyone that you recently totally lost your mind and you are more scared of your own head than you have been in years.

The next night is the *Los Angeles Times* Book Prize awards ceremony. You tend to skip things like this, but Tod and Gina have convinced you to attend. The second you're in the darkened auditorium, however, you're nodding off, startling awake. You struggle to stay focused but can't. You're surrounded by colleagues and are so embarrassed you end up hopping the seats and leaving, walking into some bar on campus where you shoot pool with a few college kids and wish you could have a drink. You think, too long, about ordering one. You have to get out of there, so you end up chain-smoking outside of the auditorium, waiting for your friends in an increasing fog of exhaustion.

There's a dinner after the awards show. You don't remember a single thing about it. Gina has to remind you, months later, there even *was* a dinner. Left to report it yourself, it never would have existed.

At this dinner you weren't exactly *at*, you're alternately strangely giddy and at other times falling asleep on your feet. Tod drives you and Gina back to her rented bungalow, where there's a guest room, where you've parked your car, making her promise not to let you drive back to the desert. You're falling asleep in the back of Tod's car, waking abruptly to crack jokes and becoming highly animated but slurring your words, and then you're out again, unable to stay conscious more than a few moments at a time. But you have no memory of any of this. You remember having visual and auditory hallucinations later on, in the dead of the night, but no memory of the dinner, of the drive back from the dinner, hours lost.

By the end of the first day of the Festival of Books, three different colleagues will approach both Tod and Gina to ask if you are back on drugs. Soon these questions evolve into rumors that you are. By the second day, Tod is being besieged by friends telling him you seem to be walking around loaded. Finally your close friend Patrick, who has spent time in San Quentin and has been an addictions counselor and doesn't pull any punches, takes you aside and asks you point-blank if you're using. You give him this—he has the guts to ask you to your face. He's one of the few people you're not mad at. You've known Patrick for years—he was one of your closest confidants after your relapse. But you've never told him what you now admit, the things you've been going through—what you've been keeping from people. He listens, like he always does. He seems to believe you. You think he'd call you on it if he didn't, but who can be sure? Who the hell knows what another person believes? You're getting paranoid, wanting to avoid everyone—you haven't done anything *wrong*, but you feel like you have.

All term long, you've been teaching several classes while slipping in and out of psychotic episodes. You've stayed on top of things. You've done a book tour. You went to the AWP conference in the middle of all this happening to your brain and body. You think you deserve a fucking medal for holding it together. You've been clean and sober for nineteen of the last twenty years, but this is how quickly all that evaporates, and suddenly in the eyes of the people around you, you are just a junkie. Your mind runs in defensive, angry loops: *If any of them had any idea how hard I work just to function sometimes, they wouldn't be talking the way they're talking.*

But how *could* they know? You make jokes all the time, without thinking twice, about how much you want a drink or an Oxy. Hardly anyone has ever heard you talk with any depth or seriousness about being bipolar. You want to hide it, yet you want people to read your mind—to know and give you credit. That's not how it works though. Once a junkie, always a junkie. A normal person gets exhausted, they're exhausted. A junkie gets exhausted, he's getting loaded.

And, of course, when you *were* getting loaded during your relapse, you told everyone you were exhausted.

What happens a week later: You are diagnosed with clinical exhaustion. A neurologist tells you it will take six months to fully recover from the taxing demands you put on your brain without knowing it. He tells you that the psychotic episodes will continue but lessen in intensity and duration if you can stick to a strict sleeping pattern: going to bed at the same time every night, and trying to get seven to eight hours; eating at the same times every day, three small meals, not the single meal you tend to eat late at night. There is no quick cure, though you're bad off enough, the neurologist says, that you could have, in the past, been sent for the "rest cure" at some medical facility. They don't tend to use these terms anymore (much like bipolar's previous name, *manic depression*), but you've had, more or less, a nervous breakdown.

Weeks later, you will tell Tod over lunch how pissed you are that no one came to you directly—that no one gave you the benefit of the doubt, and they instead turned you into some gossipy festival scandal.

"It's not like that," he says. Tod, though younger than you are, is known among his friends for being a caretaker, a paternal type. "These people love you. They just don't know how to approach something like this."

But you just want to demand, *Something like what? Something like* me?

You are tired of other people and their judgments.

You are even more tired of what you have done to yourself to earn it.

You try to listen to Tod. Try to believe that everyone's questions were meant as some form of care and love. It will be a very long time, though, before you can begin to see it this way. You still have moments when you can't, when the hurt and humiliation seize you, wanting to morph into anger. But the truth is, you know it's not anyone else's fault.

How can you tell a junkie's lying?
His lips are moving.

———

AUGUST 20, 2009: You are going to kill yourself. You sit in that shack in Wonder Valley.

You have smoked ten of your cigarettes.

Wind blows through the sagebrush and ground cover and birds slowly come back and perch on the rafters. You listen to the wind.

You've taken a few of the pills. Just to feel a buzz once more before you die.

You have not taken all the pills yet, but you know you will.

All this will be gone soon. You smoke a cigarette down to the end. You're about to flick it out the door, but instead, you blow on the cherry until it glows red and quivers small heat waves in the air. You hold it against the skin of your forearm and let it burn. You take a deep breath and try to ride with the pain. You try not to move. Try not to make a sound. You don't move until the cigarette has burned itself out on your skin, which smells sweet and smoky in the air.

You let out a deep, very slow breath. You think about lighting one more cigarette. Or maybe you will just take the pills now and smoke and wait for your overdose.

You listen to everything you can. The wind blows through the scrub brush. If you are quiet enough, you can hear the lizards on the porch. The woodpecker sound of a roadrunner's beak somewhere outside. When the wind picks up a little, it lifts and pulls at some of the corrugated metal roof. You hold your breath. You close your eyes. Pigeons coo on the support beams. Their tiny feet pat lightly on the rotting wood. The wind picks up and the wind calms. It's loud and then it's quiet, but it's never quite silent if you listen close enough. And you are listening as closely as you possibly can. You are listening. You are trying to be as quiet as possible. You are erasing you. You close your eyes and you hold as still as you can and you listen.

This is what the world will sound like without you.

ACKNOWLEDGMENTS

First, thanks to my terrific editor, Kevin Doughten, who helped me from the start to find the book within the book. I can't think of a better editor to have had for this project, or any project. Thank you for your creativity and brilliance. Also, major thanks to my great agent and, more important, friend, Ryan Harbage. I owe you. Big-time.

Special thanks to everyone at Crown Books, especially Claire Potter, who bailed me out of trouble more times than I can count and proved to be a generous asset every step of the way.

To all of my friends who read this in various stages of development: Craig Clevenger, Gina Frangello, Josh Mohr, Patrick O'Neil, and Zoe Zolbrod. Also, for her incredible support, I owe so much to Emily Rapp.

For publishing excerpts of the manuscript, thanks to *Black Clock, The Nervous Breakdown,* and *The Rumpus.*

Thanks to my mother and father for always supporting me and my career, even when I didn't make it easy. And huge gratitude always to the best big sister in the world, Diana.

Thanks beyond words to Gina Frangello, who told me I had a book when I didn't think I had one, and for being my closest collaborator.

And last, to Gayle, who was the biggest supporter of me and my career for twenty-two years. I owe you more than I can ever recount here. Thank you, always.

ABOUT THE AUTHOR

ROB ROBERGE is the author of four books of fiction, most recently *The Cost of Living*. He teaches creative writing, and his work has been widely anthologized. He also plays guitar and sings with the Los Angeles–based band the Urinals.